MW01258204

# Are you an Indigo? Discover Your Authentic Self

## Take control of your Destiny

By Dennis Michael Waller

# Are You an Indigo?

## Discovering Your Authentic Self

By Dennis Michael Waller

**Copyrighted 2010**

To contact the author: dmichaelwaller@yahoo.com
http://thedmichaelwallerreport.blogspot.com/

*renovatio-latin meaning rebirth or to be made new again*

Front cover illustration- "In two places at once" circa 1530 Woodcut by an anonymous German artist.

ISBN-13: 978-1466290969

My Children and Grandchildren
*Mike, Francesca, Ian, Vincent*

# Contents

# Prologue

Ken Small worked with me on this book. In the beginning he asked me what an Indigo was. He said he had never heard the word used before to describe someone. My mind started racing trying to come up with an answer that would make sense to someone new to the topic. It was at that moment this story popped into my mind. My answer to him was Indigos are Eagles living in a world of chickens. The issue with most Indigos is they don't know that they are Eagles. Instead they think that there must be something wrong with them because they just don't fit into the chicken world. Once an Indigo realizes that they are an Eagle and not a chicken, there is an awakening to their true nature and can begin to fulfill their destiny. Spread your wings and learn to fly!

Here is the story of the Eagle and the Chickens.

A naturalist was visiting a farmer one day and was surprised to see a beautiful eagle in the farmer's chicken coop. "Why in the world, asked the naturalist, have you got this eagle living in with the chickens?" "Well, answered the farmer, I found him when he was little and raised him in there with the chickens. He doesn't know any better, he thinks he is a chicken." The naturalist was dumbfounded. The eagle was pecking the grain and drinking from the watering can. The eagle kept his eyes on the ground and strutted around in circles, looking every inch a big, oversized chicken. "Doesn't he ever try to spread his wings and fly out of there?" asked the naturalist. "No, said the farmer, and I doubt he ever will, he doesn't know what it means to fly."

"Well, said the naturalist, "let me take him out and do a few experiments with him." The farmer agrees, but assured the naturalist that he was wasting his time. The naturalist lifted the bird to the top of the chicken coop fence and said "Fly!" He pushed the reluctant bird off the fence and it fell to the ground in a pile of dusty feathers. Next, the undaunted researcher took the ruffled chicken/eagle to the farmer's hay loft and spread its wings before tossing it high in the air with the command "FLY!" The frightened bird shrieked and fell ungraciously to the barn-yard where it resumed pecking the ground in search of its dinner. The naturalist again picked up the eagle and decided to give it one more chance in a more appropriate environment, away from the bad examples of chicken lifestyle. He set the docile bird on the front seat of his pickup truck next to him and headed for the highest butte in the country. After a lengthy and sweaty climb to the crest of the butte with the bird tucked under his arm, he spoke gently to the golden bird. "Friend, he said, you were born to soar. It is better that you die here today on the rocks below than live the rest of your life being a chicken in a pen, gawked at and out of your element." Having said these final words, he lifted the eagle up and once more commanded it to "FLY!" He tossed it out in space and this time, much to his relief, it opened its seven-foot wingspan and flew gracefully into the sky. It slowly climbed in ever higher spirals, riding unseen thermals of hot air until it disappeared into the glare of the morning sun. The naturalist smiled and thought how happy he was with his days work. Like the eagle, he had for many years, let other people define his worth and direct his life for him. Like the eagle, it had taken a life and death situation for him to realize his self worth and real calling in life.

# Acknowledgments

I would like to thank all the people out there out who have done so much work in this field. If it wasn't for their commitment to the study of Indigos, I would not have been able to put this information together.

In writing this book, I notice that the right people would show up at the right time. I wanted to do an interview with an Indigo to show you their thoughts and insight and that is when Daniel came along. My deepest thanks go out to Daniel for sharing his inner most personal thoughts with me for the interview.

I want to thank Kandice Bush for her contribution. Her story and her poetry is an example of what Indigos have to deal with and how she came to terms with the trials and tribulations of life.

Victor Trucker showed up with his incredible story of when he was 6 years old. I could not have asked for a better way to show you what the power of being an Indigo can do. Victor is a great example of what one can do when they find their life's purpose. I also want to thank David Parke for his contribution and for bringing a different perspective to the subject with his views on Past Lives and Lives between Lives. A special thanks to David Hulse who gave me permission to use his article on Solfeggio Frequencies. David is considered a leader in the field of Solfeggio Frequencies and it's an honor to have him be a part of this project.

I also want to thank my son and daughter, my Indigo children. Thank you for teaching me so many life lessons. To trust in them and let them be who they are meant to be. I can say that I have learned more from them than what I have taught them. How many times did I hear the voice of God in their laughter and happiness? Thank you!

Working on this project has been a journey. I want to thank

those who helped me in getting this project completed. A special thanks to David Knouse, Leslie Whitten, Jerry Stratton, Pete Kelly, Ben Reynolds, Michael Hall, Paula Schermerhorn, and Ken Small. Most of all my thanks to Cheryl Andrea McMillan for telling me to write this book.

And for those of you not mentioned, you're not forgotten, and know that you are appreciated and loved. Thank you.

# Foreword

Have you had the perfect life? Well, if you are human, the chances are the answer is no. But it is okay. That is the purpose of this book, to help you indentify if you are an Indigo and what you can do to start moving towards living as a perfect life as you can.

What we are going to cover in this book is what and who an Indigo is and how it applies and affects you. If you or one of your love ones is an Indigo this book will help serve to give you an understanding of what that means. By understanding this information, it will help you in your daily life. You will also find useful information in dealing with the issues of being an Indigo in the business world and in relationships. You will see the difference between being a Group Thinker verses being a Free Thinker. You'll learn how feelings play into being an Indigo and steps in how to deal with these emotions. You'll see how overcoming fear can unleash the power within.

If you are an Indigo or not, know that all you have is today. Do all you can do today. Make it count because today is all you have. That is all you will ever have, just today so make the most out of it.

My mistake in life was being afraid of making the changes that I knew I needed to make. My excuse was that I needed to put the needs of others first. I sacrificed my desires to maintain what I thought was required of me for the good of the group. In retrospect, if I had to do over again knowing what I know now I would have cast fear to the wind and took off on the life that I should have lived. I now know that the so-called concerns were nothing more than excuses to keep the status quo intact.

My advice for you is don't be afraid to make a sudden and radical change if the opportunity arises as long as feel it is the right thing to do after careful consideration. It is imperative to follow your own wisdom and inner voice especially when there is a complete absence of doubt. You must live for yourself.

Follow your heart and live life independent of the good opinions of others. It is your life to live so live it for you. Do all you can  to break free of the preconditioning that we all have been exposed to over the years. Don't live in your memories, instead go out and make new ones. Don't waste your time trying to live the life that you think is expected of you by others. Live your life for you, follow your heart.

Go and find the love of your life and do whatever it takes to make it work and don't let go of them. In the end, the money won't matter but the way you loved will. To me, that is the one thing that you are allowed to take with you when you leave this existence. That is the love you created while you were here. Time is too short and precious so don't waste another moment.

And my last thought, learn to make friends with Christ. Develop a relationship with Him, treat Him like a brother and open up to Him, you'll be glad you did. He is there waiting for you to realize He is here for you. Instead of praying for enough gas in the car to get you home, pray for Him to ride home with you. Ask and you will receive and you'll see when you believe.

If continually you keep your hope,
quivering like the willow in longing for Heaven.
Spiritual water and fire will continually arrive,
and increase your subsistence.
And if your longing carries you there, it will be no wonder.
Don't pay attention to your weakness,
but to the intensity of your longing.
For this search is God's promise within you,
because every seeker deserves to find something of which
she seeks.
Increase this search,
that your heart may escape from this bodily prison.
If your spirit shall not live without the body,
for whom is the blessing promised in the words;
*In Heaven is your Provision?*

**Rumi**

# Introduction

What's an Indigo? What does that mean? How do I know if I am one? Is it alright to be one? What I am to do? What does all of this mean? I just discovered that I am an Indigo, I am not sure what to do next. Am I alone in all of this?

These are just a few questions I get from people wanting to know about Indigos. While these may seem like simple questions, the answers go far beyond that. Most people out there that are experiencing the symptoms of Indigos are searching for answers but don't know how to find them. One way of looking at it from the perspective of an Indigo that doesn't know he is an Indigo is like having a puzzle in a box but not having the top with the picture to give them an ideal of what the puzzle is to look like, must less how to go about putting the pieces  together.

It's time to make a decision. Are you ready to take the journey to self discovery and find your Authentic Self? The only thing that has been preventing you from having a rich rewarding life is your own limiting beliefs. Overcome that today; make the decision to live a life of peace, love and joy. This book will show you how immensely powerful you are. You have the power to create the kind of life you have always wanted to have. This is the time to start.

This book was created out of my own spiritual journey in trying to figure out what life is all about and what does it mean. Consciously or unconsciously, we are all in search of the path to a fulfilling life. For me I had to get clarity in what I really wanted out of life. I searched for the answers to my own questions. In doing so, in my travels I have learned so much about being an Indigo. I found the answers that I was seeking and I learned new ways to deal with life. While it hasn't been easy, the rewards far outweigh the pain and suffering that I had to endure.

I want to share with you those lessons I have learned. I

have used some stories and examples I have come across to help illustrate the point I am making. I have also chosen a few people that exemplify what one can do when they are aware of the power they have within and use it. Being an Indigo at times is nothing more than a state of being. I hope and pray that this book will serve you well and will bring to you new ways of looking at life that you haven't seen before.

One lesson that I want to share with you now is this. If you have these burning dreams buried deeply in your subconscious that are trying to come to the surface, then let them. Learn to embrace these dreams and act on them. Don't let the rules of Group Think stop you from listening to the messages of those dreams. It is okay to live in your imagination from time to time. Give yourself permission to explore what it is that your subconscious is telling you. Remember everything in this world started with a thought in someone's imagination. This is the start to living a life free of the constraints of the world.

As with any journey there will be resistance along the way. You will question yourself and the purpose.You may meet with resentment from others for breaking away from the traditional way of thinking. And there might even be rejection from the people around you. Fear not, this is normal in the quest for true understanding and enlightenment. The key is not to fall prey to the external forces that will come your way. On any path to the truth there will be struggle and hardship, but is the price for the freedom in the discovery of your true self.

In the words of Arthur Schopenhauer,

*"All truth passes through three stages. First, it is ridiculed. Second, it is violently opposed. Third, it is accepted as being self-evident."*

Stay true to yourself and stay on the path, regardless of how narrow the path may become. That is the purpose of this book, to serve as a guide on your journey to self discovery.

To help you discover if you or a loved one is an Indigo. There is a quiz of 75 questions designed to help indentify if you might be an Indigo. Once you can identify with being an Indigo, you will find tools and strategies of what you need to know. You will learn how to deal with the issues facing Indigos and where to search for the answers that you are looking for. Even if you are not an Indigo, the information here is valuable for learning how to live the life you are meant to have.

There are two groups of Indigos. The first group knows that they are Indigos and are moving forward with the evolutionary process. The second group of Indigos does not know that they are Indigos and are searching for answers, trying to make sense of it all. This book addresses both groups. Look upon this book as a map. You must know where you are in order to know where to go. Within these pages, I hope that you will find some answers. If you are an Indigo and if so, what you should do.

**The Quiz** - I would suggest that you take the quiz before reading the book. In taking the quiz you'll be able to indentify different aspects of your life that apply to being an Indigo. After taking the quiz hopefully you'll begin to have clarity and understanding. The quiz is a list of traits and characteristics found in most Indigo's. While most Indigo's can relate to about 80 to 90% of the questions, this isn't a definitive test. However, in my experience, I have found that these questions seem to hit home for most Indigos. Consider the quiz a form of connecting the dots. Most Indigos haven't realized that these seemingly unrelated characteristics are in fact related. Before taking the quiz, I want to point out the preconditioning that all of us have grown up with and not even aware of.

We have all been taught to assume that what we have learned is above question. And, if someone or something doesn't fit into the framework of what we have told to believe as the truth, we dismiss it without a thought. So, when someone like David Icke talks about the lizard people, we automatically jump to the conclusion that he must be crazy. What I have learned is, instead of dismissing someone as crazy, I now ask myself, what caused this seemingly normal person, who has never shown any signs of being crazy, to go off the cliff with this out of bounds nonsense.

While we might believe that we are in control and have not been preconditioned to think a certain way, I ask you to do this one exercise. Next time you are on an elevator, place your back against the doors and face in toward the people. You'll know what I mean at that point. You'll feel very uncomfortable and out of place, that is because of the pre-conditioning that we have all gone through, without ever knowing it. This reminds me of the words of Rene Descartes,

*"If you would be a seeker after the truth, it is necessary that at least once in your life you doubt, as far as possible; all things Break free and live life on your terms. Think for yourself."*

What all of us have gone through in life is trying to live up to what is expected of us by others. We are unknowingly living life under the pretense of what is and what isn't acceptable to society. Here's one for you, what if they, society has got it wrong? Eh? Then what? Well, I'll tell you, you're in trouble. That is why it is so important to discover for yourself the truth and stop buying everything being sold to you at face value. I love the way Oscar Wilde put it.

*"Most people are other people. Their thoughts are someone else's opinions, their lives a mimicry, their passion a quotation."*

The first step to breaking free from the preconditioning is to question the why, the what, and the how. I wonder if you could ask the cow what he is doing following the other cow in front of him while being lead down the chute to slaughter, what his answer would be. I bet you his answer would be "I am just following him" Don't be a follower, be a leader. Break free of Group Think. Thomas Jefferson, one of our founding fathers knew this all too well. Here are his thoughts.

*"Neither believe nor reject any thing because any other person, or description of persons have rejected or believed it. Your own reason is the only oracle given you by heaven."*

The first step in anything, whether you are an Indigo or not, is to approach everything with an open mind. Learn to do your own research and come to your own conclusions. Work independently of the good opinion of others. Don't fall into Group Think, think for yourself. What you choose to believe, that is your choice. Do it on your own terms with the knowledge that you have learn. Come to a conclusion that makes sense to you based on your own thinking, not others.

I want to illustrate how powerful and at times how evil Group Think can be. Look to the Bible to see the events that lead up to the crucifixion of Jesus. There was a small but powerful group of Jewish Priests in the Temple in Jerusalem. They were threatened by Jesus while the masses love him. Seeing that Jesus could disrupt their control over the people and fearing that Jesus would remove the veil and expose their corruption they set out to campaign against Jesus. They went about spreading lies, complaining to the Romans that Jesus was a threat not only to the Jews but the Romans as well. They made promises to key people to help in the fraud to convince the people that this was best for them. Just a few men were able to turn enough people around to get Jesus killed. The sad part to this event is the masses were just dragged along for the ride in fulfilling the desires of a few.

You must break free of Group Think. It is probably the most important first step you can take when starting on the path to discovering your Authentic Self. Regarding the power of Group Think, remember these words Hermann Goering, one of the masterminds of Hitler's Third Reich. He made this statement shortly before being sentenced to death at the Nuremberg Trails.

*"Of course the people don't want war."*
*"Why should some poor slob on a farm want to risk his life in a war when the best he can get out of it is to come back to his farm in one piece? Naturally, the common people don't want war: neither in Russia, nor in England, nor for that matter in Germany. That is understood. But after all it is the leaders of the country who determine the policy, and it is always a simple matter to drag the people along, whether it is a democracy, or a fascist dictatorship, or a parliament, or a communist dictatorship. . .Voice or no voice, the people can always be brought to the bidding of the leaders. That is easy. All you have to do is to tell them they are being attacked, and denounce the pacifists for lack of patriotism and exposing the country to danger."*

Don't allow yourself to be dragged along for a ride. Make it a point to break free of letting other people think for you. Be your own person and realize the power of thinking for yourself. That is the first step you need to make on the path.

At the end of the day it doesn't matter where Indigos came from or what our bloodlines are. What matters is Indigos are here to play a key role in the physical and spiritual evolution of our planet in the months to come. The purpose is showing the others the way. So, whether or not you're an Indigo, become aware of the coming changes to our world and arm yourself with the knowledge of the universal law of Love. There are only two forces in the universe, love and fear, light and darkness, good and evil. Practice Love in your daily life and seek the truth.

You are the block of marble and the sculptor. You have the power to create anything you want out of that block of marble. You are the sculptor of your own creation. Choose well the path you take and keep your chisel sharp and your hammer handy. Here is a quote from the 3rd century Greek Philosopher Plotinus:

*"Withdraw into yourself and look. And if you do not fine yourself beautiful yet, act as does the creator of a statue that is to be made beautiful: he cuts away here, he smoothes there, he makes this line lighter, this other purer, until a lovely face has grown his work. So do you also: cut away all that is excessive, straighten all that is crooked, bring light to all that is overcast, labor to make all one glow or beauty and never cease chiseling your statue, until there shall shine out on you from it the godlike splendor of virtue, until you see the perfect goodness surely established in the stainless shrine."*

You contain everything you need to transform yourself into whatever you desire. It all begins within. It is up to you to decide how to create the Authentic You that you are meant to be.

The power is within you.

# Chapter One

## Identifying Indigos, Their Traits and Characteristics
### Being an Indigo, Traits and Characteristics

**So, what and who is an Indigo?** The term Indigo came into the mainstream in 1982 with the release of the book, "Understanding Your Life Through Color", by Nancy Ann Tappe. Tappe, an internationally-acknowledged author and psychic noticed that in her research of specially gifted children starting in the 1960's that these special children had indigo colors in their auras. Hence, the word Indigo was coined for these children that showed these special colors. Associated with the auras were character traits, personalities, and behaviors that become the foundation for what we know today as Indigos.

There are several different opinions on just what an Indigo is. While most are right to a degree, I have found that there are many ways to describe Indigos. Once you learn the qualities of being an Indigo, you'll soon discover that throughout history there have been groups of people that have had this way of thinking and understanding of the world. The first group that comes to mind is the Native American Indian. As a collective, they embodied the true meaning and understanding of being an Indigo.

The more I study Indigos the more convinced I am that the best way to describe the phenomenon of Indigos is to view it as a philosophy. Indigo-ness is a philosophy, a state of mind, a way to live. Like the Native Americans, Indigos have a sense of the big picture. Indigos know that there is no separation among living beings and creatures, that we are all interconnected.

Within the Hopi language there is no reference to temporal concepts. According to Benjamin Lee Whorf, the well known linguist, the Hopi language has "no words, grammatical forms, construction of expressions that refer directly to what we call time." To give you an example, when we see the wind whipping up the waves at the lake, we say, "Look at the waves on the lake" Where the Hopi would say, "The lake is wavy."

The Aboriginal Peoples of Australia refer to space in the manner of defining space relative to the observer. The view of time by the Aboriginal People is quite different from the Western World. Aboriginal People look at the past, present and future as happening at the same time. While they have lived in a linear time world, they don't live by it.

There are several ancient cultures throughout the world that share these beliefs. My thought is these ancient peoples were multi-dimensional beings. By having an understanding of the big picture, they knew that they were $4^{th}/5^{th}$ dimensional beings in a 3 dimensional world. This is exactly what Indigos are! $4^{th}$ dimensional beings! And this is the main issue with Indigos in trying to accept this fact. With this knowing of the truth comes an understanding of the philosophy of life for Indigos.

**Warriors and Teachers** - One aspect that all can agree on about Indigos is the fact that Indigos are here to tear down the old systems and bring in the New Era. Along with bringing in the New Era people will look to Indigos to show them the way, to teach them the path. What I have found that is very interesting is this Warrior/Teacher concept has been foretold in different prophecies.

In the late 1920's Nicholas Roerich of Russia conducted a scientific expedition to Central Asia. It was there while Roerich was in the Himalayas that he recorded the prophecies of the Buddhist monks living high up in the monasteries. It is one of these remarkable prophecies that jump out to me concerning Indigos. Here in his words is, in my mind, is the Indigo Prophecy.

*"It is told in the prophecies how a new era shall manifest itself. First there will begin an unprecedented war of all nations. Afterward brother shall rise against brother. Oceans of blood shall flow. And people shall cease to understand one another. They shall forget the meaning of the word Teacher. But just then shall the Teacher appear and in all the corners of the world shall be heard the true teaching. To this word of truth shall the people be drawn, but those who are filled with darkness and ignorance shall set obstacles. Already many warriors of the teaching of the truth are reborn. Only a few years shall elapse before everyone shall hear the mighty steps of the Lord of the New Era. And one can already perceive unusual manifestations and encounter unusual people. Already they open the gates of knowledge and ripened fruits are falling from the tress."*

With 2012 just around the corner and with all the strife in the world, one can feel a change is coming. There will be a need for Indigos to be prepared and ready to take charge of the task that awaits them. It is imperative to make haste in realizing the power that you have so you may serve to the best of your ability. Whether you are to be a warrior or teacher, you are first and foremost an Indigo, with a special gift.

**Old Souls / Being Intuitive** - Indigos are a special group of gifted enlightened Old Souls that operate at a higher frequency than the average person. Indigos are highly spiritual and intuitive. They are born with an inner awareness that what is seen and taught in the main stream media and in many religious organizations are lacking in truth.

They derive this inner awareness from having lived all aspects of life over several lifetimes. Indigos who are aware know that they are not their Ego, rather than feeling separate from the world, they know that they are interconnected to all living beings.

**Indigos being Angels** - Some even believe that Indigos are the next generation of mankind, a higher evolved human being. It has also been suggested that Indigos are Angels in a human form. Indigos are able to see past the illusions in the everyday life of this world. Either way, Indigos have chosen to come back at this time to help in the spiritual and physical evolutionary process, to help raise the vibrations of all mankind. They are here to show the way for the rest of mankind.

**Indigos and Ancient Aliens** - On the same track of Indigos being Angels, there are those who believe strongly that Indigos have different DNA. These people believe that Indigos are distant relatives of the Ancient Ones. Some think that Indigos are descendant from the Akhu, the Genesis Lords, bird-like ancestors that came to Earth to give the beast, [humans] an extra strand of DNA. It is this extra stand of DNA that provided the beast with the ability to have compassion, awareness and a soul. With this DNA also came the knowledge to ascend to a higher form of consciousness. With the Beast receiving this gift, they now became the Guardians of Earth.

This is known in mythology as "The Gift of the Feather". The first human to receive this gift was ADAMUS, son of Prince EL. Sound familiar? This line of thought could be a book by itself. Anyone interested in learning more is encouraged to check out the "Terra Papers-The Hidden History of Planet Earth" by Robert Morning Sky.

Speaking of DNA, there was a report on ABC News on July-16-2008 about the discovery of human remains of Bronze Age cave-dwellers being found in a cave in Germany. The

Lichtenstein cave is located in the foothills of the Harz Mountains in Germany's Lower Saxony region. The human remains dated back to 3,000 years ago. Thanks to the bones being so well preserved, the researchers were able to obtain high quality DNA samples. Interestingly the remains turned out to be from the same family group that had a distinctive and rare DNA pattern.

The researchers tested the inhabitants of the nearby village to see if there was a remote chance that someone would be a match. 300 locals were tested with saliva swabs as part of the archaeological research, two local residents turned out to have the exact same genetic characteristics: Manfred Huchthausen and Uwe Lange.

The men, Manfred Huchthausen, a 58-year-old teacher, and Uwe Lange, a 48-year-old surveyor, had known each other from living in the same village, about half a mile apart from each other. *"I could not believe this at first, but I think it's truly fascinating."* Huchthausen, whose family has lived in the area since the 18th century, told ABC News. He said he has received many calls from across Germany since the archaeologists published their findings.

*"People are interested to find out what it is like to be able to trace back the family roots for 3,000 years, and I can tell them, it's awesome, it's sensational, and it's fascinating."*

What this story demonstrates is the possibility that there could be ancient bloodlines with their DNA still intact today. Who is to say this isn't possible? Food for thought.

**Challenge Traditional Systems** - Indigos are here to challenge and tear down old traditional systems within our educational, political, religious, medical, nutritional, technological, family, and all fear based belief systems. With Indigos come Universal Wisdom, Divine Knowledge, and a clear vision of perfection. Their mission is to help the rest of mankind to create a new paradigm, where we all live in a world of Integrity, Compassion, Unity and Love.

**Integrity Based** - Indigos for the most part, live with integrity based on the principals of peace and harmony. They have a strong distaste for nothing but the real truth. They are able to sense dishonesty with a built in lie detector. They don't buy into the political system, much less any other system of authority, seeing the corruption within these systems. These are the reasons Indigos are unable to cope with dysfunctional systems. It doesn't matter if the dysfunction is at home, work, school or society, they cannot disassociate, nor have the ability to pretend that everything is fine. This type of action goes against their sense of integrity. After all, it is their job to bring humanity into an era of Integrity and Compassion.

**Connection to Nature** - One really special trait of Indigos is their heightened sense of awareness and natural connection to nature and the animal world. Most Indigos feel more comfortable within the animal kingdom and nature than in the "real world". Because of the Indigos heightened physical, emotional and spiritual sensitivities, they can reach a higher level of attunement with the natural world that most humans can't obtain. This is a reason why Indigos will avoid crowded places like malls, concerts, large sporting events or any other place where large groups gather. It is just too much stimulation and creates a negative energetic overload. They are more comfortable being alone, surrounded by nature or being among other Indigos.

Indigo women would rather work in their garden on a beautiful Saturday afternoon instead of going to the Mall to shop for shoes. On a rainy day, an Indigo woman will prefer to curl up on a couch wearing a cashmere sweater with a good book and their cat in their lap. Indigo women definitely prefer solitude with nature and with animals over being at a Starbucks or hanging out at the Mall with friends. Indigo woman like all other women want to look their best wearing nice clothes but Indigo women don't use it as a excuse or allow the labels of their clothes to identify them.

Another aspect to Indigos wanting and needing that connection to nature isn't as much about what they get out of it has it is what they don't see and deal with in nature. In nature there is a harmonic balance with all living things. When a person gets into nature and quiets the mind, they too will become engrained with the harmonics and frequencies of nature. Within that is a balance that is calming and relaxing. It is a connection back to the divine source, the divine intelligence of the universe.

On the other hand what is missing from nature that the Indigo enjoys is the lack of neurosis. Neurosis doesn't exist in nature. When have you ever seen a Chipmunk going to therapy because his father was sleeping around with the Chipmunks? Or seen a Beaver going to therapy because he had anger issues, or an Elm tree in therapy because he feels that he is really an Oak tree trapped in an Elm tree? Or a Mockingbird dying her feathers blue because she wants to be a Blue Jay? See how absurd these issues are when taken out of the human world and placed into nature? It is in the absence of these neuroses in nature that Indigo finds peace and comfort.

**Indigos, Arts and Music** - Indigos have a fondness for the arts. They will either be involved in the arts or have a deep appreciation for them. It is common to see Indigos in the music industry and in the arts. It is the expression of the soul through the arts that attracts Indigos. It's these deep feelings and emotions of Indigos that want to burst out for the world to see and hear. The arts serve this purpose. Indigos can be very artistic. Even if there is not a strong gift in the arts, there is a deep admiration and respect for the arts. This goes back to the gift of being emphatic, the ability to feel the soul in a song or painting. They have an ability to sense the soul of the creator in the piece of music and the message conveyed in the song. They do have a strong attachment to the arts because of this awareness.

If an Indigo doesn't feel that they have the talent to be an artist, then you'll see them owning an Art Gallery. Indigos make great authors. The funny thing about Indigos is while they may be terrible spellers, they can write beautiful prose. As with all Indigos who discover their talent, they know not where it comes from.

Another point about Indigos and music is that Indigos have a sense of being able to listen to music more from the heart than the mind. In reading a good book, they are able to pick up on the emotions of the author. In art, they sense the feelings of the Artist in the painting; the Indigos have a higher sense of intuitive of awareness in the Arts.

**Light Bulbs / Electrical Devices** - An interesting characteristic of Indigos is the inability to get things to work right like watches, light bulbs, cell phones, computers, etc. This is because of the natural heightened energy field they have. The interference with electrical items or electronics creates havoc to the point where nothing will seem to work right.

One school of thought on this phenomenon is these issues with electrical devices are cause from the energy generated by hyper-communication. This energy created within the DNA causes the electromagnetic field to intensify to such high levels has to cause this interference. There are Psychics, Mediums and Healers that are familiar with this affect. During these times of heightened awareness, the hyper-communication is experience as intuition or inspiration. This phenomenon can happen at anytime even in your sleep through your dreams.

The higher the state of consciousness is of the Indigo, the more profound the experience will be with the interference with these devices. As an Indigo works on their state of awareness and develops a higher sense of consciousness, these issues will increase along with the awareness. So stock up on light bulbs and practice patience with those devices that challenge your center of peace.

**Issues with Religion** - Indigos have a major issue with organized religion, seeing that the dogma being taught is not accurate, and is nothing more than a tool to manipulate people. This is frustrating to Indigo's as they cannot buy into the program and must question the hidden agendas. Most Indigo's have discovered that the true Kingdom lies within and no longer require the Church for their salvation.

**Indigos are highly intelligent** - Being highly intelligent, as Indigos are, they have a knowing that they are wired differently from other people. Often times, Indigos do poorly at school, because their inner sense told them that the programs being taught are lacking in the whole truth and substance. Most Indigos will score high on IQ test but will fail in the day to day grind of a structured school system. This leads to most Indigos being labeled as Rebellious, Dyslexic, Hard to Teach, Slow, even ADD - Attention Deficit Disorder, and ADHD - Attention Deficit with Hyperactivity Disorder. In my opinion, most of these issues are born out of boredom. It is known that some Indigos are placed on drugs such as antidepressants to make them appear normal. That is a shame, to drug these bright and wonderfully gifted children because of an inability to understand them.

**Indigos in Business and Dealing with Money** - Now this is an interesting area. This will make sense to you if you're an Indigo. Since Indigos see the world differently, they are not as attached to material things as others. Money and the trappings of success just are not that important to them. They don't care about having a Mercedes SL63 or having a Platinum Rolex; it doesn't hold the same meaning to them as it has to others. Indigos seem to develop a detachment from money and material things. While not driven by money, some may be sensitive to the perceived inequities in wages and salaries and do not want to be taken advantage of in the process. Indigos are more often motivated by other means other than financial security. Yes, they know they need to work to pay the bills, buy food and have a place to live but they don't measure their performance by economic incentives. They seem to see how disempowering having their focus on money is. They don't let the dollar drive them. This difference in values brings up more negative issues in the workplace. Many Indigos have a difficult time holding down a job because of the frustration of having to deal with a broken down system. The issue is Indigos don't quite understand the world around them or how to fit in. This is because it is hard for them to understand why so much importance is placed on money and beating the competition; while dishonestly and integrity are thrown out the window in the name of success and greed and corruption are rewarded. Indigos value system is in direct conflict with the laws of business, and as such, they suffer from it. For the Indigos that cave in, and shut down in order to get along, they suffer a life that is very disheartening and unfulfilling.For those who fight, they will find themselves either in charge or self employed. It's the warrior spirit within Indigos that shines at these times, when they refuse to compromise their values.

Indigos, when left to their devices will develop an extremely strong sense of Unyielding Compromise. In other words, they will not compromise their core beliefs and values, even if it means taking a personal loss. Keeping their integrity is more important than a short term gain. In business, this will cause heads to butt and conflict, but that will not matter to the Indigo. Their sense of right must prevail.

In business, when Indigos are in their element they tend to solve new problems very quickly and assertively, sometimes outside the normal framework of business practices. They tend to take a direct approach to obtaining results. They are not afraid of taking risk or trying an approach that unproved. They prefer to lead by setting an example rather than instructing others.They will come across as being more modest than egocentric. They lead by doing, not by delegating.

In the workplace when allowed to be who they are, they will be very optimistic, gregarious and outgoing. This is because other people will be unknowingly drawn to them. While these people may not know it, they will sense the strength of being around Indigos. Indigos will accept change in the workplace but first might require a good argument. Indigos are great in a more flexible, unstructured work environment. They value freedom of expression and the ability to change quickly from one activity to another. They tend to become bored with the same routine. As a result of this, they will seek other opportunities and outlets for dealing with their high sense of urgency and need for spontaneity.

**Indigos and Childhood** - Indigos have a history of traumatic childhood situations. Most have experienced extreme hardships as children, as they were raised in family situations of physical or sexual abuse. It is not uncommon for them to have lived in an environment lacking in emotional and spiritual support. For the most part, Indigos had a tough time growing up. This only compounded the problem of trying to figure out why and who they are.

Because of the issues with a traumatic childhood and other events many Indigos begin to lose their eternal soul wisdom and purity at an early age. In the chaotic environment that they were subject to, their awareness, once so pure and connected to the blissful essence of God, was disconnected. This created a feeling of abandonment, loss and confusion and led to the disillusioned view of life. The inability to fit in causes more feelings of grief, loneliness, and disappointment.

Through it all some Indigos were able to maintain a sense of integrity while others fell into drug and alcohol abuse. Many Indigos considered or even attempted suicide. Most suffered through bouts of being ridiculed, rejected and abandoned. This forced many to become outcasts, reclusive, and loners. For the most part, life was hell for Indigo children.

**Indigos and being Empathetic** - Indigos are much more intuitive and aware of their surroundings and other people. They are empathetic and can pick up on other people's feelings and thoughts. The spoken word is not as important since they have this sense of knowing and feeling. They just know. It is hard to explain, but asking an Indigo how they know what they know, would be like asking a normal person how to breathe? The first reaction would be confusion, because you just breath, there isn't any thought to it. It is the same with Indigos, they just know.

Indigos don't spend too much time caught up with mindless TV like American Idol or Dancing with the Stars. They tend to stay away from mainstream media. It only serves to frustrate them. They are drawn to entertainment like theater, standup comedy, or anything that seems to go over the heads of others. They do enjoy connecting with nature, reading and watching programs on subjects that interest them. While not too involved in aggressive sports such as football, they do enjoy other sports like cycling, running, skateboarding, or in my case, snowboarding.

There is a school of thought that Indigos are born with the gifts of clairvoyance and healing. Indigos, once aware and trained, can access the fourth and fifth dimensions of Consciousness. While normal humans operate within the three dimensions of this reality, Indigos can naturally cross over to the higher plains of consciousness. Along with being clairvoyant comes a more sensitive nature and the ability to tap into the healing powers of the divine.

An issue that some Indigo's have with being Empathic is that they might mistake the feeling of guilt instead of being empathic. This can cause a lot of problems for the Indigo. They will feel compelled to act on the false readings of self guilt when what it really is being empathic and picking up the emotions of the other person thinking that the emotions are their own. It is important for an Indigo to learn the difference between the two. While there is nothing wrong in helping someone, it is imperative that it is done for the right reasons.

**Indigos and Relationships** - Let's talk about Indigos and their relationships. This is the area that affects all of us, Indigos and non-Indigos, but for Indigos it is worse. An Indigo in a relationship with a non-Indigo is like being in a relationship where the only form of communication is through charades. You get it and they don't! The frustration of trying to get a point across is at times unbearable. It is the "Don't you see it?" situation that is hard to deal with. It is like hitting a brick wall.

While you think you are with the right partner, you still may have feelings of loneliness, sadness and desperation. You may experience an intense feeling of wanting to go home even when you are home because deep down inside you know that isn't where you belong. This is because you are not with your Soul Mate. Trust me, only another Indigo can understand an Indigo. No wonder most Indigos are either single or divorced. When an Indigo does find their Indigo mate, there isn't much need for the formality of a piece of paper to make it right.

The Indigos who are in relationships are for the most part, miserable. Their partner is making their life a living hell because of the differences between the two of them. For the most part Indigos in a relationship are learning tolerance and patience or another way to ignore a nuisance. I am here to tell you now, the ONLY way you, as an Indigo, are ever going to have an intimate, fulfilling, meaningful relationship is to be with another Indigo.

Why live a life with someone and be in a relationship that is full of isolation and discontentment? Anything else will be selling yourself short and creating a situation that will produce stress. This is a very unproductive way to live life. Continuing in a relationship like this leads down only one road and that is the road of destruction. On this road everything will be destroyed, your happiness, your life, your soul and your sanity.

Don't maintain a relationship out of convenience or because you think that is all you deserve. However, I am not saying to go home and pack your bags and leave. First, find out if this is where you belong, if not, then take the necessary action to correct it. Life is too short to sell yourself short and settle for less than you deserve.

So, what are Indigos really looking for in a relationship? How about a mutual respect and honor with an exchange of thoughts on higher levels of consciousness. They are looking for relationships where they can exchange thoughts, emotions and love; that is at such a high level of vibration and frequency that it is beyond words to describe it! During intimate times, you will not know where one person ends and another begins. Within this fulfillment of ecstasy, the two of you become one because you already are.

Every Indigo, if he or she is true to themselves, knows this truth of how you long for that Soul Mate, the one that you can explore the God/Goddess within. You know that deep inside of you is a burning desire to experience that "One-ness" with the one that you are meant to be with. That "One-ness" of one touch, one look, one heart, one soul. It is within these times that "magic" comes to be.

Because you know that this type of Love is the most powerful energy force in the universe, you will never be happy or content until you find it. Within this power is the ability to create any desire, any reality. To have this freedom to explore and express your true nature, to experience an authentic love with a partner that is your equal that is what awaits all Indigos who are able to find our Indigo Soul Mate.

So, what are you to do? Well, first off, hang in there. With this new awareness you will have a better sense of what you need to do. Be like water and seek your own level. Once you can identify with this issue, you'll be on the path to greater things. Spend time on meditation, seek out your guides. And, seek out other Indigos.

If you have been in a mess of a relationship, then it is time to clean up that mess. That includes getting rid of all that low level negative energy that you have accumulative over time. Get into the best shape you can, and I mean into the best physically, emotionally, spiritually and psychically shape you can. Clear out the old to make room for the new. You can't get to second base as long as you keep a foot on first base, so get going!

**Indigos and Past Life Memories** - Here is an area that is interesting to Indigos. For the most part due to how we were raised, we are taught that reincarnation doesn't exist. After careful research and study I have come to the conclusion that we all have lived before. Not only have we all been reincarnated over and over on this planet, this planet also has gone through it's own reincarnated. In the Hopi world and among some Physicists, it is believed that the world is on her fourth incarnation. It is more than just a coincidence of how the Mayan and Hopi prophecies talk about the fifth world along with 2012 and the sudden awakening of people from around the world in discovering their authentic selves. In that discovery is the knowledge that we all have live before and all are part of the one-ness of the universe.

What I have learned about Past Life is Indigos seem to have a stronger tenacity to remember past life memories than others. While an Indigo might not know why or where these memories are coming from, they do explain why Indigos have issues with anxiety, grief, and anger to name a few. With this said, I recommend past life regression. Within in you'll discover not only secrets to your true self but the reasons you might be experiencing some of the negative issues in your life. In addressing and facing these issues head on, you will find closure and understanding. At the very least, you'll discover that there is more than what we see, hear and feel here in this lifetime.

I have read the works of Dr. Brian Weiss, Michael Newton,

Ruth Montgomery as well as others on this subject. I was fortunate and honored to meet David Parke of New York Past Life and Coaching the Soul, & while he was in Dallas. A NLP Master Practitioner, Certified Hypnotherapist and Life Coach, David Parke was trained by Dr. Brian Weiss for Past Life Regression and by the Newton Institute for Life Between Lives. He gives workshops on past life regression and other transformational techniques across the United States and maintains a private practice in New York. I asked David his thoughts on the subject to give me a clear understanding. Here are his thoughts.

*"Approximately 30% of Americans and 60% of the world's population believe in reincarnation and for them past life regression is a very real phenomenon. Children are particularly interesting when it comes to reincarnation studies. Up until the age of 9 children don't have a strong critical faculty, which is one of the reasons that they are so creative. The lack of this critical faculty gives many children direct access to their past life memories. Many times when we think that a child is playing "make believe" or talking with imaginary friends it is possible that they are simply acting out memories from previous lives."*

*"Dr. Ian Stevenson spent a great deal of his career traveling the planet following the stories of children who were reincarnated and had vivid memories of their past lives. He conducted interviews with the children, their families and the families that the children said they belonged to prior to their death. He wrote a number of books on the phenomena of reincarnated children and pioneered research regarding birthmarks and birth defects and how they corresponded to the manner and mechanism of death in a previous life."*

*"There are a number of theories in the past life and life between life communities about Indigo children. Many of the prevailing beliefs are that Indigos are "old" souls. My experience has been somewhat different. I find that Indigos typically fit the patterns of "hybrids."*

*"A hybrid is a soul that has spent a number of lifetimes on planes other than Earth. In life between life studies, most notably those conducted by Michael Newton, Earth is considered to be just one of many planes that souls incarnate on in order to grow, learn and evolve. The density of Earth creates a challenging environment and souls that have recently come from other planes are most affected by it. Hybrids are known to be extremely gifted but also far more sensitive and tend to face a number of psychological and physical health issues. This tends to run more parallel to what many Indigos experience."*

I'll address the issue of Hybrids for those of you who are unfamiliar with the term. Anybody who has followed the work of Ruth Montgomery will know what David Parke is discussing here. Also, the work of Hugh Everett's Many Worlds Theory on Parallel Universes will show a belief in other planes of existence for living beings. Even in the String Theory in Physics lays out the foundation for other worlds, for other planes of existence, all in existence at the same time. What David is talking about is the souls that have lived or have lived on these other planes. This isn't any more farfetched than the thought of flying machines just a few centuries ago. I'll go into more detail later in the book in the Metaphysics section. But for now, let's get back to Past Life Memories.

Throughout your past lives you may have experienced numerous physical and emotional traumas, some of which may have a profound effect in your current life causing major problems. What past life regression is a set of techniques that uses focused trance to uncover unresolved memories from a single past life or a number of past lives.

Anxiety, grief, fear of loss, and anger are a few of the emotional issues of Indigos which may be resolved with past life regression. Indigos as well as Non-Indigos with allergies and chronic pain have also experienced profound relief when those conditions have been tied to past life trauma.

Past life regression can help you indentify and stop the cycle of "habitual" behavior and provide you with new tools and healthy resources to empower your life. It is a relearning of past mistakes that you get the benefit to learn from.

There is also Life between lives regression. In discovering the meanings of life between lives, you could learn your purpose and why you're here. You could discover why you meet resistance and obstacles in this life. For some life between lives regression can help bring this knowledge and awareness to you. In a heightened state of awareness you will be able to learn your soul's purpose and answer many of the questions that may have been bothering you.

Life between lives regression was pioneered by Michael Newton of the Newton Institute. He found that clients from all walks of life were reporting the same experiences upon their physical deaths in past life regressions. After years of work and thousands of case studies he reported his findings in two books, *Journey of Souls* and *Destiny of Souls*. I would recommend reading these books to learn more about the subject.

A life between lives regression will help you transcend your everyday existence and connect you with your authentic self. The answers are available and life between lives regression can help you discover the reasons you are here. Life between lives regression is just the beginning of a wonderful journey of integration and understanding.

In taking to David he shared his belief that the souls of Tibetan Monks are being reborn all over the world. It is both of our experiences that more enlighten souls are being reincarnated at this time. There is a heighten sense of a divine presence. There is a reason for this event. There is a spiritual awakening taking place on a global scale. The pieces are being put into place for a mass change. There is a desire in people wanting to reconnect back to the divine source. A new age is upon us.

# Chapter Two

## Thoughts on Staying on the path for Indigos

*"It ain't about how hard you can hit. It's about how hard you can GET hit and keep moving forward. How much you can take, and keep - moving - forward."* —Rocky Balboa

Along the way there are a few things you can do to stay on the Path. Study these suggestions and practice them on a daily basis. Keep a journal to mark your progress. Find what works best for you and get a routine together and follow it. You have got to have a road map in order to know where you are going. Above all, never lose sight and give up. It is not about getting knocked down. We all get our butt handed to us from time to time. It is about getting back up and moving forward. Stay the path and always keep your eye on the reason and purpose.

**Become mindful of your thoughts**. Hold a vision of the life you want and who you want to share it with. Create an image of the perfect mate. Get into the details on the qualities that you want in your mate as well as the physical features you desire in them. Make a list, get into it and list everything you want. Ask better questions to get better answers. This is true in determining what you want in a mate. In asking yourself questions, you will come up with answers that will paint a picture of who it is that you really desire to be with. Now, ask yourself who you must become in order to attract this person. Become committed to becoming the person you need to be by making the changes now.

Do you need to clean up a few areas? Do you need to practice compassion, patience, and understanding? Are you overweight and wanting to attract a physically fit partner? Do you want a neat and organized mate while you live in chaos? Indentify what it is that you need to do to transform into the person that your ideal mate would want to be with. Focus on who you need to be and who you want in your life. Write it down, make a list, set a timeline to it and start now, Keep this vision in your mind. Keep your thoughts on the positives and don't let negative thoughts take over your mind. When these negative thoughts try to invade, remember to stay on the path and focus. In the words of Gandhi, "You must become the change you seek. "

Change your thoughts and change your life. It doesn't matter how unsuccessful you have been in the past. Begin today to work on the disciplines and habits that will bring you into the world you desire. Work on your character, for character is destiny. Just stay on the path, live in peace and the right person will appear. I hope that you find the right partner and have the relationship that is meant to be. Know that your future partner is looking for you too. You deserve it and they deserve it. So get busy!

**Belief, Faith, Desire -**

*"Since Belief is all important, it behooves you to guard your thoughts; and as your beliefs will be shaped to a very great extent by the things you observe and think about, it is important that you should command your attention."*
—*Wallace Wattles*

**Belief, Faith, and Desire.** The difference between belief and thought is the belief that failure will be manifested, will be done to you as you believe. It is important to know that it is in the quiet mind that things get done. You must sincerely believe that you have a right to whatever you desire. You must remove all doubt and fear and any negative thoughts that might still hang around. Whatever it is that you desire is already here. But you must start with a belief that you already have it. To have a belief is to know that it is real. You must realize that in the act of belief is where it all begins. In order to start the process of manifestation, you must know what you feel, and what you attract and what you imagine you will become. In this belief, you will activate the cosmic intelligence within you. As you believe, so you will be.

**Belief** - While on the subject of Belief and Faith, I want to share with you the power of Belief as describe by Bruce Lipton, Ph.D. Lipton is one of the pioneers in the study of DNA and has an incredible understanding of how DNA works. In his book, The Biology of Belief, Bruce Lipton writes that life isn't control by your genes. His discovery was that life is controlled by belief. Before writing his book, Bruce Lipton was teaching Cell Biology at the University of Wisconsin's School of Medicine. Due to his amazing discovery, he resigned from the school because he felt what he was teaching was the wrong approach. He realized that the universe and the human body are both interconnected in a spiritual and mental nature. It is in this invisible field of energy that controls the functions of the body. He found that you can impact and alter your genetic structure by changing the way you see yourself. Your perceptions have the power to change your genetic makeup, your beliefs can and do control your biology. Lipton learned to understand that our own personal belief system has the capacity to change our world, a very profound statement. Please check out his book, *The Biology of Belief*.

**Faith** - You've wanted to change your life but it has not been easy to do so. You look at your responsibilities and the expectations that others have of you and that depend on you. I know, it is tough not knowing what direction to go in.

This is where faith comes into play. You will need to step out on faith in order to move into the life of joy and fulfillment. Follow your passion, get clarity on what it is that you care most about and have passion for. Learn to trust your inner voice. Have Faith that the laws of the universe will deliver unto you as you believe. Begin to think from the perspective of eternal wisdom and know that you are free from the chains of this world. In this freedom you will become aware that fear, lack, poverty and distress are only states of mind created by the mind. If there are times that you have doubt, ask this simple question. Is this action taking me closer or farther away from my goals, purpose, and passion? You'll know the answer. Have Faith in yourself, surrender to the cosmic consciousness and know that all your needs and desires are on their way. Don't forget to give thanks and give peace to all that comes your way. Once this is mastered, you will know the serenity of living connected to the source.

**Desire** - Quiet your mind and contemplate the life you desire. Create an image of this wonderful life and who is in with you. Imagine the circumstances and the environment that you see yourself in. Make this image as real and vivid as possible. Make it so real that you can taste and touch it. Now hold that vision in your mind. Visualize this image as if it already exists here now. Believe in it. Feel the confidence of this vision. Know that it is real. As you believe and desire it, so it will be manifested. Remember this 3 step mantra to creating anything in the universe - Make Believe, Believe, Know.

**Protect Yourself** - Another strategy is being mindful of staying clear of anyone who is operating at a very low vibration or who is very negative. Protect yourself from the negative energy of other people. These types of people will only serve to bring you down and get you off the path. It is next to impossible to protect yourself from these negative energies of these people. Let me put it another way, Stay Away from them! Look at the ten negative emotions listed later in the book. Keep them in mind with dealing with people. When other people exhibit these emotions on a regular basis, find a way to stay away from them. If you do need to deal with them, keep it simple and short.

Do your best to surround yourself with people like you who come from a higher level of vibration of love and understanding. Being with these people will only reinforce your own harmony and keep you grounded. Remember this one law. "If you want to know what level you are in vibration with, just look at your immediate surroundings." Resonate at the highest frequency you can by being around those who are already there.

**Keep an Optimistic Attitude** - No matter what is thrown your way, keep an optimistic attitude. You are not your surroundings. You are not your circumstances. I know this can be rather difficult to do but you must keep yourself in positive thoughts and positive emotions. Emotions have a way of working out in your mind how to overcome and discipline you. Negative emotions are not through repression or suppression. Rather when you repress a negative emotion, the energy grows in your sub conscious mind. If you really want to transform your life and yourself of negative emotions, you must watch what you think about and choose to control your mind and rid yourself of negative emotions. Only from a state of peace, love, and joy will you be able to keep at the highest state of vibration. It will be within this highest state that you will see the manifestation of your thoughts and dreams. It is a universal law that like attracts like. By keeping in this state, you will see like minded people showing up at the right time. It will be in this environment of positive, rational, loving people that will help keep you in a proper state of mind. Remember, it will be from this state of mind that the people you desire will appear. The universe understands feelings and emotions. It is the building blocks of all life. In order to attract the person of your dreams, your frequency must match up to what it is that you desire. Keep your thoughts, feelings and emotions in the state of goodness and you will see the effects of living in a balanced and happy life will provide. Remember you have the right to choose the life you want.

This quote from Muhammad Ali drives home the point,

*"I know where I am going and I know the truth, and I don't have to be what you want to be. I'm free to be what I want."*                                            — *Muhammad Ali*

This is where having an unyielding sense of compromise comes into play. You have a God given birth right to be free to choose your own density. So choose to be healthy. Choose to be successful. Choose to be prosperous. Choose to make a difference and be the best that you are meant to be. Your sub conscious mind is subject to the thoughts of your conscious mind. Be aware that whatever you choose in your conscious mind in a convincing manner will become reality. If you are not where you would like to be, then shift your focus from your old habits of thinking and choose to dwell on the life you want and deserve. And above all else, be faithful to the You that you wish to become. Change your thoughts and keep them changed and your destiny will change.

**Meditating** - I am going to start with a quote from John Stuart Mill. Mill was a British Philosopher during the 1800's and made an impact on several issues that still affect us today. I chose this quote because it best describes my thoughts on meditation. Meditating isn't confined to be being done in a lotus position. You can meditate while washing the dishes; it is more about getting into the right state of mind. Here is what John Stuart Mills had to say about meditating,

*"Solitude, in the sense of being often alone, is essential to any depth of meditation or of character and solitude in the presence of natural beauty and grandeur, is the cradle of thought and aspirations which are not only good for the individual, but which society could ill do without."*

One way of staying in a higher state and entering a state of peace is to meditate daily. Daily meditation is required to maintaining balance. In meditation you can reconnect to the "Oneness "of the cosmic consciousness. You can get that direct experience of wholeness and awareness within the silence of meditation. It will provide a recharging of your centering to peace and love. In meditation, you will reclaim your deep inner peace and bliss. Be in the moment of joy and bliss within the unconditional love and peace of the source. Let the divine cosmic energies flow through you. Let go and surrender to all that you have been hanging on to. You know in your heart what you need to let go of and discarded. Follow your heart.

You can meditate in several ways. For me when I am feeling out of balance and frustrated, I get back to nature to find that inner peace. Even if it is a city park, I find taking a long walk through the woods to be very beneficial. Taking a hike and getting away from the city and the noise can refresh one's soul. Get connected to nature and concentrate on the surroundings and see the beauty of the masterful work of the universe.

Be silent and listen to your inner soul. In the quiet still moments of meditation, in the reflection one's self, one can find solace, peace and understanding. This alone will raise your level of consciousness and vibration. What a great way to clear out one's mind. This type of meditating reminds me of a quote from Sidney Lovett,

> *"Every now and again take a good look at something not made with hands, a mountain, a star, the turn of a stream. There will come to you wisdom and patience and solace and, above all, the assurance that you are not alone in the world."*

I want to close with a quote from Paramahansa Yoganada on meditating. As you can see, the power of meditating is universally known.

---

*"The soul loves to meditate, for in contact with the Spirit lies its greatest joy. If, then you experience mental resistance during meditation, remember that reluctance to meditate comes from the ego; it doesn't belong to the soul."*

## Be more present and live in the moment!

*"You cannot act where you are not, you cannot act where you have been, and you cannot act where you are going to be; you can act only where you are."* — Wallace Wattles

Learn to give full attention to the moment. Open yourself to the experience without judgment. Don't let distractions break the connection between you and the moment. If you are in a relationship and when you are with your partner, commit with your entire being to being in the moment with them. By living in the moment and focusing on them, you will create and attain a level of spontaneity, understanding, and attraction that is incredible. This will only increase the meaning of the experience. Living in the moment will make you both more aware of how incredible and special your love is.

**A story about living in the moment** - This beautiful heartfelt story comes from Thich Nhat Hanh, the World Renown Buddhist Monk from Vietnam. I can't think of another person that has attained a greater level of Spirituality and Enlightenment than Thich Nhat Hanh. He embodies the meaning of an Indigo that knows their path and purpose. I was moved deeply when I read this story. In it, you'll see the simplicity of life and how one can see the face of God in  the most humble of places when you are living in the moment. It is all in how you choose to view the world. The question is do you really see when you look? It is being aware of the moment, in being able to really see. Please read this story and take away from it the importance of being aware and living in the moment through the eyes of a child as well as an adult.

"Vietnam has extraordinary rainstorms. One day, I sat by the window of a friend's home and watched a scene I could have watched forever. Across the street was a low-roofed dry goods store. Coils of rope and barbed wire, pots and pans hung from the eaves. Hundreds of items were on display - fish sauce and bean sauce, candles, and peanut candy. The store was so packed and dimly lit; it was difficult to distinguish one object from another as the rainstorm darkened the street. A young boy, no more than five or six, wearing a simple pair of shorts, his skin darken by hours of play in the sun, sat on a little stool on the front step of the store. He was eating a bowl of rice, protected by the overhang. Rain ran off the roof making puddles in front of where he sat. He held his rice bowl in one hand and his chopsticks in the other, and he ate slowly, his eyes riveted on the stream of water pouring from the roof. Large drops exploded into bubbles on the surface of a puddle. Though I was across the street, I could tell that his rice was mixed with pieces of duck egg and sprinkled with fish sauce. He raised his chopsticks slowly to his mouth, savoring each small mouthful. He gazed at the rain and appeared to be utterly content, the very image of well-being. I could feel his heart beating. His lungs, stomach, liver, and all his organs were working in perfect harmony. If he had a toothache, he could not have been enjoying the effortless peace of that moment. I looked at him as one might admire a perfect jewel, a flower, or a sunrise. Truth and paradise revealed themselves; I was completely absorbed by his image. He seemed to be a divine being, a young god embodying the bliss of well-being with every glance of his eyes and every bite of rice he took. He was completely free of worry or anxiety. He had no thought of being poor. He did not compare his simple black shorts to the fancy clothes of other children. He did not feel sad because he had no shoes. He did not mind that he sat on a hard stool rather than a cushioned chair. He felt no longing. He was completely at peace in the moment. Just by watching him, the same well-being flooded my body.

A violet shadow flitted across the street. The boy looked up for an instance, his eyes startled by the blur of bright color, and then, he returned his gaze to the water bubbles dancing on the puddle. He chewed his rice and egg carefully, and watched the rain in delight. He paid no more attention to the passersby, two young women dressed in red and purple *ao dai*, carrying umbrellas. Suddenly he turned his head and looked down the street. He smiled and became so absorbed in something new, I turned to look down the street myself. Two young children were pulling a third child in a wooden wagon. The three did not have a stitch of clothing on and were having a grand time splashing in the puddles. The wheels of the wagon spun round and round, spraying water whenever the wagon hit a puddle. I looked back at the boy on the doorstep; He had stopped eating to watch the other children. His eyes sparkled. I believe my eyes reflected his in that moment, and I shared his delight. Perhaps my delight was not as great as his, or perhaps it was greater because I was so aware of being happy.

Then I heard him call out, "Coming Mama," and he stood up and went back into the shop. I guess his mother had called him back in to refill his rice bowl, but he did not come out again. Perhaps he was eating with his parents, who scolded him for dawdling so long over his first bowl. If that was the case, poor child! His parents did not know he had just been in paradise. They did not know that when the mind divides reality up, when it judges and discriminates, it kills paradise. Please do not scold the sunlight. Do not chastise the clear stream, or the little birds of spring.

How can you enter paradise unless you become like a little child? You can't see reality with eyes that discriminate or base all their understanding on concepts. As I write these lines, I long to return to the innocence of childhood. I want to play the Vietnamese children's game of examining the whorls of a friend's hair- "one whorl your allegiance is with your father, two whorls with your mother, three whorls with your aunt, many whorls with your country." I'd love to make a snowball and hurl it all the way back to Vietnam. "

**Be more patient** - It has been said that patience is the path to understanding. This could not be truer in relationships. Become patient enough to give them time to voice their viewpoint. Don't interrupt their statement. Hear and understand what it is that they are saying. Don't be afraid to ask questions if you don't understand or disagree. Almost all conflict comes out of not wanting to agree or understand. Share your perspective and let them know that while you might disagree with the subject, it in no way affects the relationship. Ask yourself, does he or she, whom I love deeply, feel that I hear and appreciate them at this moment? Be fully present and aware of them and let them know that they are loved and appreciated. Practice being patient and quieting your mind around those whom you love. Master patience and gain understanding.

**Be more purposeful** - Being purposeful begins when you realize that everything matters. When you live in purpose, relationships thrive, and the decisions you make in your life will be born out of wisdom. Without purpose most people go through life and their relationships without much attention to creating anything remarkable including relationships. Learn to focus on purpose in the relationship and think about building it as much or more than any other facet of your life. Like everything in life, creating an outstanding relationship begins with deciding to do so.

When you understand that every action matters purpose will come to be. Ask yourself how you can bring more joy and happiness to yourself and your love one. Take the time to think about how to improve your relationships and how to make them as great as possible. Look to the universe and see the beauty in the interconnectedness of it all. It was all born out of purpose. Everything in the universe is in relationship and works in harmony. So, why shouldn't you? Take time to reflect on how relationships have improved along with the other facets of your life. Reinforce your want to be purposeful with the success that it has brought you. Developing a permanent purpose to improve your life as well as those around you will lead to love.

Victor Frankl said it best with these two quotes,

*"Love is the ultimate and highest goal to which man can aspire. "A man who becomes conscious of the responsibility he bears toward a human being who affectionately waits for him, or to an unfinished work, will never be able to throw away his life. He knows the "why" for his existence, and will be able to bear almost any "how."*

Don't allow other people to take advantage of you and gain control over you. Refuse to contribute to others selfishness and possessiveness. Give no one the power to deter you from your goals. Negative criticism cannot affect you without your consent. Emotions follows thought and you have the power to reject any thoughts that might affect your emotions. If it disturbs you, then dismiss it immediately.

Remember you control what and how anything affects you. Do not respond negatively to the criticism and resentment of others. Do not make comparisons. The entire process of getting angry takes place in your mind. Realize the process and when you sense it starting, stop it. You are in control of yourself and remember that!

**Being alone and being in Love** - One point I want to make here for Indigos is this. Being lonely and being alone are two completely different issues. One lesson for Indigos to learn is that you must master the capacity to love yourself. If you can master the art of self love then your relationships will flow with ease. Being alone, content and happy in oneself is critical. Only those who can exist in this state in solitude can be capable of loving, giving and sharing relationships. I know this sounds like a paradox but stay with me. In the solitude and being alone in love and happiness, you are able to love another without the need to possess them. By having absolute freedom for yourself, you are able to give absolute freedom to your love ones. Your happiness cannot be taken away from you nor will you want to take your partners happiness from them because the happiness originates from within. You will have that state of happiness with or without your partner being there. The depth of sharing is unbelievable along with the joy and happiness with this mindset. Without being dependent on each other for love, there is more love. There is no fear of losing the love since it comes from within.

**Dealing with and Prioritizing your Problems** - This is a simple process that can bring a sense of peace back to you when you are becoming overwhelm with problems. The first thing you should do is to identify and prioritize the problem. Ask yourself if this is a 5 minute, 5 hour, 5 day, or a 5 week problem? Is this problem going to matter a week from now, a month from now? Most of us get worked up over problems that really don't matter. When you are in the middle of problems raining down on you, take a step back and evaluate the situation. In determining the scope of the problem and realizing that it isn't that big of a deal, you'll be able to approach the issue with calmness. Now this does require that you approach a problem with the perspective of finding a solution. Coming from a perspective of blame will only compound the magnitude of the problem. Practice common sense in dealing with problems. To borrow an old saying, "Don't worry about things you control, because if you control it, then you can change it. Don't worry about things you don't control, because no amount of worry will change it. So don't worry."

**A Technique for staying Centered** - I want to share with you this technique in staying centered that works for me. First, I want you to get a clear image of the life you want to have. Imagine the serenity, peace and harmony; imagine the place where this is. Whether it is the beach, the mountains, it doesn't matter, what matters is where you see yourself in this ideal setting. Create the details to fill out the vision. Imagine whatever your heart desires to fulfill the vision. Imagine yourself in this setting with the feelings of love and peace surrounded by what brings that sense of serenity to you. Make this vision as real as if it is already here and you can go it at a moment's notice. Contemplate this vision until you can recall it in an instance in your mind. Make it real in your mind. Practice till it becomes a part of you.

Some people might call this going to your "happy place" and that might be one way of putting it. I have noticed when people are talking about a past event with vivid detail and passion; it almost seems as if they are reliving it while telling it. We have all these memories where in the recall we are taken back to that time and place. While retelling the event we are able to recapture the feelings of that moment. Those memories are usually implanted with such feeling and detail because we were in the moment at the time the event was taking place. When we are in the moment we are more aware of everything around us and connected to the surroundings.

This is precisely what you need to do to create that internal state of serenity. You must create that same sense of awareness and passion in your vision to get to that state in an instance. You must believe in this vision and know that if you can imagine it, then it does exist. So get lost in your imagination and create a vision without any limits. Remember that whatever you create in your imagination can be the foundation of what you'll see in this world. Imagine it, create it and believe in it with passion. Make your vision real.

Now, whenever you are getting off centered or when things

are getting out of control, go inside yourself and focus on this vision. Feel the serenity and peace, the warmth of the loving sun, the sand between your feet. Feel the timelessness of the passion and compassion of being there. Just a few moments in this state will bring a sense of calmness back to you again. No matter what comes your way, remember that this too will pass but you will always have your place of serenity to escape to. Practice this little mental vacation and discover the power of being refreshed without ever having to leave your chair.

**Getting Centered with Mandalas** - Another technique that you can use to get centered is using mandalas. Finding mandalas shouldn't be hard to find online or at your local bookstore. If you are having difficulties locating them, please feel free to contact me. What I like about mandalas is the concentration required in coloring one. You will without realizing it become quiet and more centered as you focus on the work. Let your mind run free with the choice of colors that you use. Map pencils work great but whatever suites you will be fine. Mandalas have been used for ages by several different groups of people including the Buddhist and Hindu. The reason these work so well for Indigos is the relation of concentric design and geometric patterns of mandalas to sacred geometry.

Mandalas are used by Buddhist to aid them in meditation. It is a sacred place for them to focus their thoughts into spiritual ritual. You too can tap into this power. Carl Jung, the famous Psychologist, used mandalas to indentify emotional disorders in his personality and has a tool on his path to wholeness. Jung considered mandalas as "a representation of the unconscious self."

The symbolic nature of mandalas can serve to access deeper levels of the unconscious while at the same time facilitate creating a meditated state to experience a sense of oneness. What a great way to get away from the stress of the world and rediscover your inner peace.

**A Method for Dealing with Stress** - Here is a perspective of looking at life that works great in dealing with stress. Learn to operate from the end. What does that mean? It means to imagine everything you do as it has already happened. Create in your mind the ideal life that you wish to have lived. In other words, write the obituary that you would want written about you. Write the ending with all the details that had happened in your life. Think of all the good times along with the bad times that you dealt with peace. Recall the wonderful relationships that you had. Be the friend that a friend would want. Have an image of the lives that you touched and improved. Consider it a fulfilled blessed life. Get a clear image of what you want your life to look like when your time is done here.

No matter what you are dealt, look at it as already completed. If it is an assignment at work or writing a book, look at it from the end. Imagine that whatever it is, it has been completed. What this does is separate you from the stress of dealing with an unknown. This frees you to focus on the task on hand instead of the stress of how you are going to get it done. Since you know the outcome, you can deal with the present without fear or stress.

Look at it like a football game and knowing the score at the end. Now imagine that since you know that you are going to win the game, how would you manage dealing with a 4$^{th}$ down in the second quarter? Since you know the outcome, you wouldn't let the current situation get to you, would you? Of course not, you would take it in stride. This is the way you need to approach life. Treat everything as if you already know the outcome and relax in knowing that no matter what comes your way, you can deal with it and have the knowing that in the end, you will win. With this insight of knowing the ending, there is no stress. Act as if you know that in the end, it all comes out the want to you wanted it to be.

**Indigos and Labels** - This is one area that all Indigos

will get to at some point. As you grow and continue on your path on self discovery. You will begin to notice that the labels that have served to indentify you will become meaningless. As you rise above the illusions of everyday life, you might even grow to resent labels. While you are a man or woman, short or tall, black or white, it will not matter because the truth of knowing that this incarnation is nothing more than a role in a play. You will find yourself, when being asked your name, replying, "People call me Michael" instead of the old reply of "my name is Michael." You will become more in line with this phrase, " I am that, I am " as you will know the real meaning of it. Here is a quote from an Indigo that hit upon the subject rather well,

One of my favorite quotes is, "I am not a human being having a spiritual experience. I am a spiritual being having a human experience." That statement sums it up for me. I would go even further as to not identify myself by gender, race, nationality, or citizenship. I believe that all those labels can do is separate us from one another. For me, to separate myself using those categories is violent. Not sure if that makes sense to anyone else, it is just my opinion. :) I also think that we Indigos are not a different breed. We still eat, breathe, love, and hope, just like everyone else. We just have our "on" button lit up. With our knowledge, comes great responsibility. There are a lot of people's buttons that need to be lit up. Some people harder than others. It is an exciting time to be here!"

**Internal Peace** - The first thing you should do is get back to Internal Peace. You have probably had a tough time with life over the years. The words horrendous, frightening, and terrifying might describe some of the ordeals that you have faced. When we are beset with these negative emotions such as anger, frustration, hurt and pain, we withdraw into ourselves and close down our hearts. In reality we create the separation by focusing on the events and people that cause these emotions. We have taken away from ourselves the peace that we seek.

With this awakening that you are an Indigo, you no longer need to look outside yourself for that peace. Once the desire for peace is in place, then the means for finding peace will present itself. One way to get on the path toward peace is to become the peace you seek. When you give and extend peace, peace will find its way back to you. I like this quote from Ralph Waldo Emerson, while not exactly about peace it certainly applies to the subject,

*"It is one of the most beautiful compensations in Life that no man can sincerely try to help another without helping himself."*

And another quote from Black Elk on peace,

*"The first peace, which is the most important, is that which comes within the souls of people when they realize their relationship, their oneness with the universe and all its powers, and when they realize that at the center of the universe dwells the Great Spirit, and that this center is really everywhere, it is within each of us."*

Get back to the center within yourself where your soul resides. There if one so desires can get into a state of peace. In a state of Peace, suffering eases, conflict diminishes, pain seems to go away. In a state of peace one can quiet the mind and know God, in the stillness one can contemplate. In peace comes a gentleness, bliss, harmony, joy and happiness. In peace comes truth and clarity. In this state none of the negative energy of the world can affect or touch you. In this state you are one with God.

Only you can return to the place where peace dwells. It is up to you to recall that peace you think you lost. With this recognition that your thoughts have created this separation, you can begin to accept and forgive the events and people that have caused these emotions. Once you are able to start this process, you will break free from these illusions of separation. You'll once again open your heart to the love, peace, and joy that as always been there. In the opening of your heart, the healing will begin. You have the right to choose how to spend every moment of your life. Choose Peace, Love and Joy!

*"Indigos and the Road Less Traveled — "Two roads diverged in a wood, and I — I took the one less traveled by, and that made all the difference."*
— Robert Frost, "The Road Not Taken" 1920

As an Indigo you will find yourself taking the road less traveled. You will find peace in the solitude of the lesser traveled path. With the confidence of knowing your purpose, you will not be as concerned if situations come together or become unraveled. No matter what comes your way, you will know and understand that it is meant to be.

Another reason you would choose to take this road less traveled, is that you will lose interest in what the masses think or do. You will find yourself avoiding the low energy levels of the masses. You'll prefer to take the other route to avoid them and the "Group Think" mentality that is so prevalent today. What is accepted as news won't matter that much, because you get the big picture. You will shy away from any distressing news and will want to return to a more pastoral setting.

Another reason for taking the road less traveled is in part to your empathic nature and your ability to detect the fraud of deception in the news and in people. You will cringe at the news of suffering of not only people but wildlife as well. Your empathic nature cries out for the injustice being carried out against humanity and the planet. You will become angry with the lies being touted as truths in the main stream media. With all the pain and suffering, you will want more than ever to escape from it all, back to the river and trees. It is in the environment of nature that you will find solace and peace.

As a new way of seeing the world unfolds, you'll see the deceit and lies everywhere. You'll despise the cement jungles and what they stand for. You'll loathe what man has done to nature in the name of progress. In these moments, you'll want more than ever to get away from it all and get back to the rivers and trees. You'll want to live your life free of those who lie and steal. You'll want to spend your days in peace and solitude walking along a sunlit path, feeling the warmth of the sun on your skin as a breeze gently blows your way listening to the song of the leaves dancing in the trees. That is the road less traveled.

Those who are caught up in the illusion will not follow you. They will always take the safe route, and never stray too far because of their pre-conditioned fears. They could not endure your path; uncertainty and fear are their chains. No wonder you'll want to get away.

It won't matter what other people say or think. You know that you are making a difference. It doesn't matter if others see it or not. You will be satisfied with your inner knowing. You will develop this type of thinking while on this path, "It doesn't mean that much to me to it mean that much to you." And, you know what? It's okay.

# Chapter Three

## Indigo Children

**Indigo Children** - I want to briefly cover the subject of Indigo Children. Most of the questions I receive from parents deal with what to do with their children. They seem to have lost control over them and feel frustrated. The parents are at a complete lost on how to handle them. By the time they find me, they are at their wit's end. I know it can be tough dealing with Indigo Children. I have two! One of the first rules about raising Indigo Children is not to have too many rules. The more rules you have, the more they are going to break them. Keep it simple and practice common sense. Have trust and faith, it will be okay.

The issues I hear the most about are that the children are out of control, rude, selfish, lazy, defiant, rebellious, and head strong. The children on the other hand often view their parents as stupid, cruel, out of touch, and being tyrants. At first glance, this just isn't an issue with Indigo Children. This is an issue that has plagued parents for generations. The real issue here is the failure of the parents to understand and respect their children. While these problems are centuries old, they are magnified with Indigo Children.

One of the biggest issues with Indigo Children has to do with school. I see a lot of Indigo Children are labeled as being ADD or ADHD. Most times this is brought on due to boredom and not because of ADD or ADHD. Find a way to challenge them and to find their interest. Once an Indigo Child has found their calling, they are off and running.

Here are a few traits of Indigo Children. They interact with unseen people, spirits, angels or animals. They often speak at a very early age or not at all because they could communicate telepathically. They seem at times to talk in a way that is years ahead of where they are. Have at times a wisdom that is beyond their years. They are very drawn to natural objects, like crystals and plants. Seem to get along with animals very well. Seem to be their happiest when connected to nature. They have paranormal abilities. Photographs showing them surrounded by unusual lights, mist or orbs. When playing, they tend to sit in geometric shapes, like in a triangle when there are three or in a pentagram when there are five of them playing.

If some of these traits describe your child, then she or he might be an Indigo. In dealing with these children keep in mind what it is like for them. These children are at times scared to death. They don't know what to believe or how to interpret the world around them. They are trying very hard to make sense out of it all and at times feel lost and alone. They are having a difficult time in coming to terms with their gifts. It is not only your responsibility to be their parents but also be their guide in their transformation into adults and coming to terms with being an Indigo. This comes down to a mutual respect. In order to create an environment of respect parents will need to offer guidance, tolerance, patience, and love. Become more of a guide and consular over being a traditional parent.

One of the hardest issues parents have with Indigo Children is to allow them to make their own mistakes. Let them do what they can for themselves. Resist taking over their every move. They need to learn from mistakes the consequences of their actions. Give them the freedom to figure it out problems on their own. Instead of giving an order, give them an option. For instance, instead of telling Matt that he is going to wear a certain outfit for school, let him pick out a couple of choices and work with him to select the best for both of you. Remember, you are dealing with an old soul that is trapped in the body of a child and doesn't quite understand the why or how. This is where the respect comes into play.

Remember Parents your children chose you for a reason. They are here to help you as much as you are to help them. You have as much to teach them as they will teach you. You are their guides in this world. Treat this has a gift and a blessing. Show them how to look at the world with wonderment and grace. Show them to respect all living creatures and beings. Teach them to be nonjudgmental. Practice with them the value of tolerance, patience, and acceptance. Teach them and practice the meaning of responsibility and accountability. Don't shield them from the truth. Honestly is the rule, trust in them, they will be able to handle the truth. If they ask a question, give them the answer. Embrace their talents and encourage their interest in whatever subjects that excites them.

Together you are on a spiritual journey. Practice harmony and tranquility, remember they are divine souls. Become a safe harbor for them in this chaotic world. Let them know that no matter what the world may bring, there will always be a safe place for them with someone there that loves and understand them. Teach them how to attain serenity. Give them the tools to discover being spiritual and let them find their way.

**Victor's Story of being an Indigo Child** - Victor Trucker is a Certified Professional Life Coach specializing in spiritual awakening. Victor is located in Colorado and works with people from all around the world. His website is www.perfect-oneness.com, I encouraged all of you to check out his website. There is an abundance of information on his site. He seems to have answered just about any question that you may have about his services and the meaning of being on a Spiritual Path with a Coach. I also recommend reading his blog post, as they contain a wealth of information pertaining to Indigos or anyone who has a desire to find their path.

He is there to help people who are seeking a better understanding of their spiritual being. He helps people to locate and recognize their authentic self. He shows them that they are the answer to their every question, the solution to their every problem and the resolution to their every conflict. This allows them to find real inner and outer peace, joy, harmony and abundance that will fulfill them throughout their life.

Victor wants to share his philosophy of Peace with all of those who wish to receive it. The potentials within each of us are limitless, and the more individuals that understand this, the better for the whole world. This knowledge will soon enrich all mankind, and our self-imposed ills will vanish into what we call the past.

Here is a story about Victor and how life was for him as a child. In this story you will see how an Indigo can interact with a sense of understanding about life that is beyond their years. I hope this brings a smile to you as you see the wisdom in this 6 year old boy.

I was brought into this form in a small suburb of Minneapolis Minnesota called New Hope. From a very young age my mother knew that there was something different about me. This never changed. By the age of three, I was picking out my own clothes and showing a creative artistic side of myself that would stay with me even until the present day. By the time I started kindergarten I had already learned to read and write. It seemed that symbols and patterns came very easily to me.

Oddly enough, in sight of this, I didn't find school engaging at all. I found very little interest in what the classroom environment had to offer. Needless to say I didn't do too well in school due mostly to my lack of conformity. I found little interest in most of the toys that were popular in that day, and in fact preferred to sit for hours in my sandbox in the back yard and carry on lengthy conversations with what appeared to be no one there but just me and my playful imaginary friends.

It was around the age of six that I had my first confrontational run-in with organized religion. My brother, whom was two years older than me, had started catechism classes to prepare for his first communion, and the church my family attended hosted Sunday school classes at the same time as the catechism classes were in session, so my mother insisted I attend. After a few weeks of child Bible study we were given a simple quiz to see if we were absorbing any of the materials offered. On this particular quiz there was a question that asked: Jesus Christ was: A. Man  B. God  C. Spirit, to which I circled all three. While one of the Nuns was retrieving the quizzes from us she noticed my answer to that particular question, and brought it to the attention of the Priest leading the class. The Priest walked over to my seat and proudly stated something to the effect of, *"Young man, you have answered this question incorrectly, you must circle only one answer, you have circled all three."* I replied, *"But you taught us that he was all three."*

I think that must have embarrassed him, because he then looked around the room at all of the giggling children, and then looked down at me and asked, "If you are so smart then can you solve this riddle, If God is all powerful, can he create a rock that he himself cannot lift?" Without any hesitation, I replied, "Yes, He created your heart, which is so heavy with sin that He cannot lift it to Heaven." There was far too much silence after this, and then he asked me to leave the classroom, that I was a disruptive influence, and that my sassy mouth would not be tolerated. It was at this time that my mother intervened and took me by the arm and marched me out of the room and to the car where I sat waiting for my brother's catechism class to be released. After that incident I simply refused to have anything to do with organized religion.

My relationship with public schools and most formal regimented left-brained learning institutions didn't change very much over the years, and this put me in a somewhat awkward position with regard to society. Although I was certainly smart enough to earn straight A's, I found no interest in rote memory and reciting back what passed for facts or useful information, but behind which was little or no expressed meaning. I loved to watch the grasses and trees swaying in the breeze. I loved to watch the flowers and the birds, oh, how I loved to watch the birds. Everything you need to know about this universe, you can learn from a flower or a bird. Nothing is hidden from us except for that which we choose not to see. Since I was somewhat of a fringe dweller, I only had a few good friends throughout my school years, but they are good friends, and still are to this day. Most of the children didn't seem to want to talk to me as I didn't know how to make small talk. I wanted to talk about cosmic-unity, universal law and the illusory nature of our perceived existence. Not your typical schoolyard conversations. Even though it was the sixties and seventies, those that I knew weren't very interested in any of that. So I mostly kept it to myself.

Nearing the end of high school all of that began to change. During my junior and senior years most of the kids that never wanted to have anything to do with me began approaching me for advice. Imagine my surprise; they were actually interested in what I thought now. They were asking me for advice on relationships, issues with other students, problems with classes and extra-curricular activities. You name it and there was someone who had a question about it, and there I was giving what amounted to exceptional advice on subjects I conceivably knew nothing about, but it was good advice. I realized immediately that this advice wasn't coming from me, not this little person walking around on this little planet, but from that which sent me - that which held me in focused manifestation. It came from the same place my answer to that Priest, so many years ago, came from.

**My Indigo Children** - It is only fair for me to share with you a few stories about my two Indigo kids and what we went through together. Both of them are in their 20's now and living their own lives and I must admit, doing better than most their age. While I didn't know about Indigos when they were young, I did know that they both blessed with a wisdom and knowledge that was years ahead of most kids their age. At the time I had no clue where it came from.

One of the things that I did with my son and daughter was to embrace whatever their interest was. If they became interested in a subject because of something they seen in a movie, we would put it on the list and on our weekly library nights we would check out the appropriate books. I encouraged and supported their interest because I recognize that this was a form of learning. I could see how exploring and researching a subject give them the answers they had. At an early age both of them did not buy much they saw at face value. I had a respect and appreciation for their questioning of the things they saw. It was a learning experience for me too. Embrace and guide your children, the rewards are worth it.

Both of my kids have this wit and confidence about them that at the earliest age was well beyond their years. There are two instances that stand out in my mind. When my son was 13, he was spending the summer with his grandparents. Along with Mike were several of his cousins enjoying their summer vacation. On one particular day his grandfather came home and discovered that there was some beer missing from the refrigerator. The grandfather called the boys into the living room to find the culprit. On hearing the news of the missing beer my son spoke up and said that he could clear his name as he had proof that he did not take the beer. His grandfather stated that he should share this proof with everyone. At that moment my son said, "I can prove that I didn't take the beer, because it is not my brand of beer! " This is when the grandfather could barely contain himself from busting out laughing, he promptly sent all the kids outside and sit down in disbelief murmuring something how the heck did he come up with that. Even today several years later, the story will bring a smile to his grandfather's face.

Another time I was in our living room looking at a bottle of gin located in the wet bar. I always kept the wet bar stocked for entertaining guests even though I didn't drink. I was in deep thought on how this bottle that I had never opened was over half empty. In fact after thinking about it, I never got to open any of the bottles of gin that I had bought. About that time my daughter was walking through the living room when I mentioned to her about the mystery of the missing gin. Her response without turning around or missing a beat was, "Dad weren't you 17 once?" I mean, how do you respond to that? It was neither an admission nor a denial. It wasn't an answer but yet it spoke more with unspoken words than had she tried to come up with an excuse. In the moment I remember laughing to myself and marveled at the wit of a question being answer with a question. How I wondered where and how she could convey the answer without admitting guilt. These are just a few examples of the wit that they both displayed as kids. This is to be expected from gifted Indigo Children. Sometimes it is what it is and you just have to let go and let it be. Enjoy these times and relish in the marvel of youth. But there were more serious times with them. I feel that I need to share these with you to get across how important it is to recognize how wonderful the journey can be growing together with your Indigo Children. Keep in mind what I said about they have as much to teach us as we have to teach them.

I noticed that my daughter after watching a particular movie or show would become empathic towards the theme for whatever reason. One such movie was The Pianist with Adrien Brody that came out in 2002. The plot of the movie is about a Jewish Pianist named Wladyslaw Szpilman in 1939 Warsaw that plays on the radio there. At the outbreak of World War Two, Szpilman sees his world collapse around him. The conditions for the Jews in Warsaw began to deteriorate rapidly as their rights were taken from them. Szpilman like most Jews is rounded up and thrown into the Warsaw Ghetto. Szpilman escapes from the Ghetto and spends the rest of the war in hiding. During this time Szpilman witness the horrors that were committed by the Nazi Regime. Widespread killing by beating to death and the burning of Jews was witness by Szpilman throughout the war. The shear brutality that Szpilman witness cannot be put into words nor is a way to begin to describe the horrors that he seen. But even in the mist of darkness, there was a silver cloud for Szpilman.

The irony of all of this is was the kind act of compassion by Wehrmacht Captain Wilm Hosenfeld. The captain discovered Szpilman in hiding above the headquarters of the Captain's command in one of the vacant buildings in Warsaw. When the Captain found Szpilman, he brought him down into a room that had a piano. During questioning Szpilman, he discovered that Szpilman was a pianist. Looking at the piano, the Captain told Szpilman to sit down and play something. Where Szpilman, only a shadow of the man he once was played a piece by Chopin. Captain Hosenfeld agreed to let him live in hiding while bringing him food from time to time till the end of the war. It seems that the German Capitan and the Piano player had a common love for playing the piano. Either way, it was out of this compassion for a fellow human being that Szpilman was able to survive the war. On a side note, isn't it funny that after 65 years of this happening, we are still acknowledging the act of kindness by Hosenfeld towards Szpilman? After the war Szpilman went to great lengths to clear the name of

Wilm Hosenfeld. In the end the captain died in a Soviet Union POW Camp before Szpilman could save him. This is a great story and movie. The role that Adrien Brody played in this movie won him the Academy Award for Best Actor and it was well deserved.

**Back to my daughter** - I noticed how much the film impacted her. It was obvious that the movie had a profound effect on her and had disturbed her deeply. She seemed to have a knowing that this story was based on fact. I did not know at the time we watched the movie that the movie was based on the autobiography of Wladyslaw Szpilman. She became very troublesome and concerned about the plight of the Holocaust. She could not let go of it. Day after day it dwelled on her. After seeing the impact on her I decided to do something. What we did was made a list of all movies dealing with the subject of the Holocaust and started to watch them all. We even found foreign movies about the Holocaust and watch them too. I also went out to find books on the subject whenever I went to a book store. Her main reference guide became a book called the "Holocaust Chronicles" This telephone sized book became the starting point on researching the subject in depth. It was amazing how she just drink up the information and had this sense of things before reading or seeing them. At the time, it seemed to me that as crazy as it sounds, she was looking for closure of some type. There was a need that needed to be filled. Instead of dismissing any of this as just some crazy teen interest, I followed through with her on her journey that she needed to go on. I didn't judge the motives or the why, rather I became her guide and her partner with her on her journey.

Now what I believe is this. Whatever the reason, she was in her own way in deep sorrow and grieving for a time and place in history. Whether it was a past life memory that needed to be addressed or just a strong empathic nature, it doesn't matter. What mattered in the end is she found the peace she was seeking for. This is an example of being there

Are you an Indigo?

in a larger role than being a parent.

Here is another story about my daughter that illustrates the unyielding support that Indigo children need from their parents in their search for their purpose. Both of my kids from an early age showed signs of being very artistic. With my daughter it started with joining the band in elementary school. She began with the clarinet. I bought the clarinet for her to start in band. From there it moved to the piano, then to the guitar and bass guitar, which again I bought. While she showed talent, there wasn't that burning desire to pursue it. Then it was off to art. She wanted to get into art so off she went. I started her off with all the necessary supplies to get her going, which I paid for. She did very well, showed talent but again, there wasn't that burning desire to pursue it. By now she is a sophomore in high school and wanted to get into photography. All she had to do to get the class and join the school photography club was get the necessary equipment. And again, we are off to the camera shop to buy everything needed to get it going. I know what you are thinking, how much can one guy spend before saying enough is enough already? Or, sounds like you spoiling her by giving in to whatever she wants. But let me finish this tale. By her senior year she place second place in a national photo competition. Along with taking second place was a handsome scholarship to a major university. Plus her work was shown at a Gallery in Dallas. That was a good day for me, the day she won the competition. The day of her showing at the Gallery, that was another good day for me. You would not believe how proud I was of her for what she had accomplished in such a short time. By the time she was 21 years old she was a successful free lance photographer with her work being published. One of my clients at the time was looking for a photographer, I mentioned her and she got the assignment. At the age of 21 my daughter was working for the same client as I was, except she was making more than I did. That was another good day for me. The sense of pride in seeing my daughter succeeding in life and surpassing her father was unbelievably satisfying.

I don't tell you these stories to impress you. Rather I tell you these stories to impress upon you the importance of being there and supporting them in their search for their purpose. It is imperative for you to be more than just a parent. You must be more than that; you must be their guide in their journey towards self discovery. You need to operate from a perspective of being non judgmental in your actions. Don't give up on them, keep at it. Whatever hardship you have to endure will melt away in an instance when the payoff comes. None of the cost will matter at that time. Do not cheat yourself out of those precious moments. They are rare and far in between, so savor those moments. It is within those moments that you witness your child coming into their own. That is the reward. Live with and through your children.

# Chapter Four

## Profiles of Three Indigos - Interview with Daniel of Doria

Daniel is a young man, mid 20's living in the UK. Daniel's life has been filled with tragedy, pain and suffering. He has gone through more than most of us experience in a lifetime including a car accident that almost cost him his life. He considers his near death experience a blessing. I did an interview with Daniel and you too, will see how this young man has learned to deal with the tribulations that life has thrown at him. This is an example of an Indigo who is awakened and aware. I want to share with you his insights and views on his life that make him see things the way he does.

I first ran across Daniel in 2009 while looking at the headlines on David Ickes' website, DavidIcke.com, David had posted a video of Daniels, "Raising Eden #6 War on Consciousness "about awareness and awakening. The video was intriguing and interesting. I followed up by going to Daniel's YouTube page. I was so mesmerized with his work that I watched all of the videos that he had posted on YouTube.

Daniel has done a series of over 60 videos called "Raising Eden "that range from 6 to 10 minutes each. This series covers just about every topic and shows the interconnectedness of everything in the world. No matter how far apart things are in the world, either through time or distance, Daniel is able to show the connections. Since doing the Raising Eden series, Daniel has moved to producing other projects such as Singularity and Transcendence.

I was amazed at the depth and level of knowledge and understanding that this young man has achieved. His work prompted me into contacting him, to find out what made him tick. What I found was someone that understands the big picture, someone that gets it. I was interested in what made Daniel see things the way he does and asked him to share with me his thoughts. Notice throughout the interview his level of confidence and belief in himself, there is no fear, it is amazing. He was more than happy to answer my questions. He has given me his blessing in sharing this with you.

**The interview -**

**Dennis -** I found you through David Icke when he posted one of your videos, "Raising Eden #6 War on Consciousness, "to his website. I was impressed with the work in the video along with the information that you have gathered. I took the liberty of posting this video to my blog, to give people a chance to see your work. I just want to say thanks.

**Daniel -** Wow, Cool, I did not know that David Icke was using my work. Thanks for the heads up my friend. Thanks for your efforts. Keep up the great work Matey; you help inspire me to keep going.

**Dennis -** What would you like for people to know about you?

**Daniel -** BE LOVE - Awaken to Your Multi Dimensional SELF. It is by no means an irrational fancy that, in a future existence, we shall look upon what we think our present existence, as a dream. Intuition is The Consciousness that is being phased out at all Cost's. Do not allow this to happen. Live heart, BE LOVE and good journey to SELF.

Love is my Religion. Appreciating different angles & tactics. Being different is not a "crime", staying in your own integrity being appreciated for your talents. We do not have to agree on everything, as long as we do not impose or hijacking other channels to force 1 issue or 1 group *(demonizing & generalizing)*.

We need a different kind of unity against tyranny. We can inspire & motivate each other in so many ways, KEY is: allowing each-other to be different as complementary forces helping the network to counter any abuse & distractions of the real issues.

**Dennis** - What got you started on this path?

**Daniel** - I had an interest in the paranormal and was fascinated by it. Then, basically I knew there was a lot of crap going on in the world that could be solved but it wasn't being done, I heard words, but no action. Then I realized there are elements who don't want to solve anything, and create the opposite. So I dug deeper and then I realized everything I ever believed was a lie, so my journey inward started. I came full circle in my awakening to other streams of knowledge and I learned all KNOWLEDGE comes from WITHIN the heart itself, so not only is that where I go to for my knowledge, but also as my measuring stick and guide.

I then had my UFO experiences and encounters/sightings, paranormal experiences. And I learned various techniques for altered states by conscious will alone, by self reflecting on myself and introspection.

I broke my back and nearly died and escaped death, this reminded me of the peace inside myself also and the old me died in the crash. Then I had a deep spiritual experience where I saw my SOUL. Either my soul/god or an angel in the form of a large sun in a place of peace beyond time and space. My zero point, after seeing it, it is the route of my Creations for I have seen it personally. I try to flow this energy from within into this world as best I can and each day BECOME more of that which I already am inside. When I returned into body, I realized that is was me.

So this gives me the inspiration in life to do all my creating, death is an illusion. Why, because I have heard it? No because I have experienced it and am aware of this higher aspect of what is inside. Eternally conscious.

I want to be a positive force in the world, to inspire to create new domains of knowing, the likes of which have never been witnessed or seen before in this world. If even one way is created in doing things a better way, then great. My job is done. And I aim to inspire others to do the same, by sharing my journey and the wisdom and teachings I have gained along the way and that which I've been made aware if. That about sums a lot of it up

**Dennis** - Can you tell me more about the event that brought about the near death experience?

**Daniel** - My friend was driving, we were coming back from some clubs/bars in Skegness in Lincolnshire England and we had a car crash, he hit 3 bumps in the country road consecutively, it was night time, oh yeah 10 years before at exactly the same time at the same hour on the same day my bros best friend died in a car crash also. Anyway back to this, he was not speeding and we went down the dyke at 70 mph.

I was knocked unconscious and the car was on fire, I awoke upside down pinned to the roof by my seatbelt upside down, I slowly lowered myself to find my back broken, I checked for people but no one was there, only the shouting of one of my friends. I looked forward ,then the back and found an escape route out the back window as all the glass had been shattered, after this, I slowly kept my back straight as I went out the back window up the dyke slowly keeping me back straight.

I then laid carefully at a safe distance from the car on fire and waited. Here I felt the most immense feeling of peace as I knew I was safe and had been at a dark moment in life.

The rain was lightly spitting, cooling me and I felt the warmth of the fire crackling in the distance in my heart and the shimmering of orange shining from a distance, the warm color and crackling of fire, the night sky and stars has always brought me great comfort even now.

I then had recalled other moments of peace in my life; I had always wondered where this great feeling had come from. Then a few months later I had my zero point experience and I recognized that this place is our HOME, the place where we are really from. Peace within is the same feeling and I use it to create my work now, as my guide and as my rod of measuring the world. The place of peace and Love charged conscious living energy, vibrant and beautiful, peaceful, centered balanced, PURE LOVE and ecstasy =] bliss charged love.

**Dennis** - Can you enlighten me on the "Zero Point "?

**Daniel** - You rise high in consciousness to a high frequency unto a plane within yourself, in a dimension in the space between spaces in the same space, dimensions of light and space I suppose, unto a zero point realm at the heart of US, you can feel it even now between us, yes, that peace, that is ever present yet intangible.

A realm where you exist in many places at once and in the form of a giant sun of light a lot larger than ours, but it does not hurt you to be close to it. The sun is alive, it is you; you are alive in many clustered consciousness around it also, in many places at once. It is a realm of total peace, beyond space and time. They have no meaning there and are illusions. Conscious eternal living energy. Bliss charged beautiful pure love.

When I came back to my body my ears were still shaking and had a ringing in them, I shot up in bed and said to myself WTF was that lol. And the ringing remained for a minute or two. This was physical and was just another state of my being.

What set it off was I felt my mind drifting just before I fully woke up and so I surrendered to it without fear and I ended up in that place.

We can tune in and out of the many dimensions at will with practice and relaxation, we are like tuners, like tuning in and out of radio stations and can become any state we wish, and this is the gift of humans, Multidimensionality.

**Dennis** - Tell me more about your experiences with the UFO's

**Daniel** - The first UFO experience, it was the last day of year 8 at school 1996 round about. It was a very small fast triangle that shot out green bursts of light just before each quick powerful fast move. Dipping in and out of trees and travelling at lightning speeds at will, my friend was with me. Another encounter a year or two back I saw many red orbs for over 2 hours, first just one and then many blinking doing a light show for me. Some of my family and my sister and her boyfriend were witnesses also.

The best one is a close encounter with a VERY VERY large Mother Ship of some sort. Very eerie and no man made thing is this big, no way. In fact the biggest thing we have would not even fit in one of its lights and it had many of them flicking on and off at various stages! My father was with me.

Are you an Indigo?

All these UFO experiences I was in heightened states of excitement before I had them. For example the triangle was last day of term, I was excited. The orbs, I had been reading and had grown a lot spiritual that day I felt with reading, and then I saw that.

The third time, the Mother Ship, I had just left university for Chrimbo so was happy to be back home; it was on the way home that I had the encounter with me dad.

So I cannot rule out my own conscious as being linked directly to these events manifesting. The red orbs for example are $4^{TH}$ dimensional movement. We must ask what characteristics did these have toward me myself and what purpose would they serve to further me in my own growth? How can I use this experience to improve myself is what must be asked? Where they come from? Why and who is in them? If such things do control them, it is irrelevant for now.

**Dennis -** At what age did you become aware that you were different or had these gifts. You mentioned your family a few times. Do they have these gifts of insight too?

**Daniel -** He he I do not know exactly what Gift you are trying to pinpoint, but I will say We all have infinite potential and have an unlimited amount of things we can do, There are so many various gifts a person has that they only need to become conscious of that which is already within themselves, trying to pinpoint just one gift is really a lost cause, there is an infinite amount of variations that crop up when exploring your own consciousness and you cannot label them and try to make boundaries. So learn to be more fluid, Be AS WATER instead of solid defined boundaries in your thinking. We are all equal, and ONE and infinite in all directions like matter really is. So we all have the Gifts. It is just in energy terms what you put in, you get out, right? This not only applies to spiritual matters, But all aspects of Life:D. Response - ABILITY upon all levels for yourself is the KEY. Master yourself and you will surely MASTER the world. Do not let the world tell you who you are, how far u can go. BE MORE than the world.

About my Family, he he, Half of my family have had similar Conscious experiences as what I have had and the other half have not. I would say my family is like a perfect balance when it comes to this stuff. If I had to say a side that is most mysterious though it would be my Mother's side, things definitely run in the family on that side :).

**Dennis** - What brought about the need to get the message out and to use YouTube?

**Daniel** - I was always Open minded. I always had a passion for film/editing too and also FELT the soul of music in its differing forms. The universe is Music; everything is vibrating because energy itself is the Movement of Consciousness so this passion is really built into us all, for it is Us.

After coming full circle in my awareness of the world and its mysteries, really the mysteries of myself up to that point and how I unconsciously chose to perceive the world. I eventually decided there was not a series that really pulled everything together into one place for others to get the BIG PICTURE Quickly. so to Use my Great inbuilt creative ability  and imagination and passion for these things, I set about on my journey by taking a first step, I pulled these passions together into one and Created Raising Eden to Express it.

**Dennis** - Where do you see your work heading?  What do you see yourself doing in the future?

**Daniel** - Expanding upon my series and becoming more refined in my abilities to express my inner self and energies more potently. Raising Eden was really more about a starting Point for me and making a blueprint. They say ART is mans message to himself, I guess this is a message to myself and a Guide for me too. I see myself Writing Books Later on, and Some Radio, I have been asked already to be on radio a few times, maybe even doing some lectures. But I will definitely be heading into a more public active role in the future when I have balanced all my life aspects into ONE, that is just a part of My story that is yet to Be.

I Will Balance all aspects of my life into ONE and BEcome a leader as we all must seek to BE. There Is No Limits to what I am going to do, so watch this space... :D Whatever I do from now on though, know it will last for all Time...Raising Eden had been translated into around 4 languages which is great to see, I just would like my work to have a positive impact. To motivate people into action and Inspire them to CREATE themselves and take an active role in creating the positive reality in which they want to see. In the future I would Love to see Networks of people, organized, and free. And eventually Communities of like minded free thinking creative individuals living together outside the Corrupt SYSTEM. Even if I have changed One life which I know I have, will make me happy. Because I have already achieved this Goal, I am a very happy man right now.

**Dennis** - I know I need to wrap this up, any final thoughts?

**Daniel** - Thanks for the Interview via email, I have loved it. It is great to look back in time like that to see exactly what I said and have experienced and see that no amount of time will change any of it. My perspective has only refined in the language and how I express, it is slightly different but the core will always remain true. Thanks Dennis and all the best my friend. Good luck with your future work.

I will also continue with my works also and when I am not working, is when I am refining what I have already acquired to be able to express it more clearly for all.

Thanks for the Inspiration my friend; it is always a pleasure to meet like minded people who are on their own personal journey. For in the end we are ALL really on the same journey going to the same destination. :), that is also why it is so good to help all and share everything we have openly. Through helping others we are helping the real SELF. Which includes ALL THINGS.

Thanks for the opportunity to speak and express myself through Your work my friend.

*"Good Journey to Self and Be Love!*

This concluded my interview with Daniel. I hope this candid visit will shed some light on the inner workings of an Indigo. It is amazing the level of confidence and lack of fear he has. He certainly isn't afraid to get out there and say what he feels needed to be said or do what he feels he needs to do. In his own way, he is touching several people around the world. His first YouTube page had over 2 million hits before being replaced with his new page. At this writing, he has over 2,000 friends and over 1,300 subscribers. His story resonates with many. Reading the comments left on his page, one can see that he is not alone. I hope all of you check out his work.

**Indigo Poetry by Kandice Bush** - Kandice Bush found me. It is funny when you are on the divine path how the right people appear at precisely the right time. I wanted to do a piece on the artistic introspective qualities that Indigos have. I did the interview with Daniel but wanted a different perspective to add to it. That is when Kandice came into my life. After reading some her poetry and reading her profile that is below I was deeply touched and moved. I knew that I had the person I was looking for to balance out the introspection of Indigos. In her writings you will see several Indigo traits. You can sense the pain, agony and the frustration that she has gone through along with the feelings of being lost and abandonment throughout her life. Spending time with her, it doesn't take long to see how empathetic she is. She has that knowing of who is real and who is trying to mislead her. Now she is on the path of self discovery and knows what and who is. She is a very beautiful woman. She is a gifted and blessed Indigo. The lessons she has learn from life are being expressed in her poetry. In her words of poem one can feel the pain and agony along with her in those moments that inspired her to write from the soul. This is something that all Indigos can relate to at one time or another.

I asked Kandice how she would wanted me to present her in this book. I asked her to give me in her own words what she would want to tell you, what she wants the reader to know about her, here are her words,

"Hi Dennis, in regard to the book, my life has been full of drama & pain yes. But it has helped to mold me into whom I am & who I'm supposed to be. As rough as some of it has been I wouldn't trade it for anything. One of the biggest driving points for me in life is to be able to help others with the experiences I've gone through. To help bring them light, love, peace & enlightenment. It's what brought me to share such personal things as an eating disorder, depression, physical & emotional abuse....sometimes we don't feel we deserve any better. I was one of those people for so long. It

Are you an Indigo?

85

finally clicked that this life can be whatever we want it to be. There's so much beauty, so much to experience. I know my work might make me come off as quite depressed but it really couldn't be further from the truth. I'm quite in love with life. With all the knowledge & beauty life as to offer how could one not be? I tend to be quite the introvert. Self diagnosed with avoidant personality disorder. My writing has become an outlet for all my pain & negative emotions. I've always thought I felt things on such a deeper level than most. This negativity is not who I am in person. I just needed somewhere to put it all. Thanks, Kandice"

I am grateful for her contribution and her excitement to work with me on the book and I encourage all of you to check out her web site.

**Kandice Bush** - I figured after some recent feedback on my work it was about time to reintroduce myself. First I want to thank anyone who has ever stopped by to read my writings & anyone who has identified with even a line from one of my poems. It means more than you'll ever know. I guess I'm writing this because I feel the constant need to explain myself so I'm not misunderstood. (Thanks to a... no longer friend for pointing that out) it's funny how sometimes all you need is an outside perspective to help you see things you normally wouldn't, or even in a different light.

Also because it's been pointed out to me that I tend to compartmentalize my feelings. The dark parts & sadness in me goes into my writing. I guess this must make me look like quite the cutter. That couldn't be further from the truth. I'm an extremely peaceful happy person, quite in love with life. I love being me. My writing comes from my life experiences. Heartbroken & losing friends left & right these days. Sometimes my work appears quite morbid & full of self pity. I'm really not that way at all. Being a Libra & constantly trying to keep balance every part of me has to go somewhere. It seems I just feel things with much more intensity than most.-Kandice Bush

**Ramblings Of An A.P.D. Poet by Kandice Bush -**
I've never been one of those people who could talk to anyone. I tend to be quite shy & even introverted at times. A lot
of that comes from my diagnosis of Avoidant Personality
Disorder. Feelings of inadequacy & the fear of being judged
or rejected can be so overwhelming it affects me in every
aspect of life. Ironic, isn't it? Painfully lonely yet at times
paralyzed with fear to the point where all I do is keep to
myself. It's kept me from living most of my life, social situations, and job opportunities. It almost seems like I've never
even looked at life the same as everyone else. Then again,
perception isn't reality. I always felt... different... Like I was
just on some other level; not saying that I'm better than
anyone by any means. How do you get used to feeling alone
in a room full of people? Maybe it's the same thing as being
nervous, as being nervous is a selfish energy because you're
making the situation all about you. So I've been told any-
ways. If we as humans are "programmed" to need other people, why is it so hard to admit that? To reach out to another person for comfort... Probably the same reason why I
can't bring myself to sleep in my bed when my daughter
isn't home. The couch is the perfect size & there's no extra
room to remind me my love is over 1,000 miles away.

I've been struggling to find purpose in my life. The best
thing I've been able to come up with is I'm here to share my
stories with others, whether it be through my poetry or my
new found need to splay myself here for the world to see. To
offer comfort, hope, empowerment. With the craziness I've
been through I could write a few novels I'm sure. An emotionally unavailable alcoholic of a "father", a 5 year abusive
relationship with my daughter's father, not to mention I'm
an ex meth addict & have issues with bulimia as well. Pain
builds character. I am survivor, never a victim.

**To.get.her.**
    Libra moon rising in a mute requiem,
    neath the blur of stars crashing,
    Brought to my knees,

I wept of the darkest sins.
He laughed like he already knew my hands were dirty.

## When colors move.
In the shallow beatings of restless hearts~
Silent desperation...reminiscent of passion~
Where love means more than breath~
Meet me there.

## Sumatra.
I remember in a moment of mosaic frailty,
under a charcoaled spring moon.
when all of me ached for him,
& the irises whispered his name,
in every part of my heart he was written on.

Wide eyed & dressed to the nines.
I had walked into this dream,
with a slenderly strut.
Clouds parted in the sky,
until his lips met mine,
& the heavens collided.

*"She took the pieces of him that has him missing from
himself & all I got was the lukewarm leftovers numbing
my lips on a 1,000 mile flight.*

*"But I love him!" I screamed in my head, Reality's arms
pulling me away."*

Daylight burns my eyes,
The walls are closing in
as I wake up alone
without him
Again.

## Refraction of The Tides.
Woven into transcendental realms
my lazily made halo breathing ether into
    broken vessels

He smiles like the summer winds that swept me

Heart singed
& curved to the silence of the night
that's where you'll find me
etched in the burning breath echoing cross my lips.

## Bring Me A Thousand Scarabs.
I used to imagine him & I alone
under Egyptian tides
fingers tracing hope in waves of passion on my back

I gave him all of me

I am formless
molding in his hands
wordless
my gasps pleading "love me..."

Tonight I cried like the stars were bleeding
because the less he's around
the more I get used to it
& the more blackened their light becomes
The tourniquet I fashioned out of erasable ink
    promises for my soul
is now ripping at it's liar's seams
& the desert is left whispering of my heart

## Humming in the tones of black
on the darkest nights I bleed poetry
from the tourniquet mouths of deaf muses
d(r)owning colors
under the melting dusk of a lithium skyline

I wear of a needled heart
sorely stitched to bloody sleeve
crudely fashioned
under a disfigured grace
smoke red
& voiceless

**In the beauty of tragedy**
"sweet little alchemist..."
he whispered
"did you always believe that butterflies were white?
phantom tipped?
& singed with the solace of love?"
"sometimes."
I sighed
"sometimes the sparrow's breath kissed my lips
& I forgot this place wasn't heaven."
it's unsobering...
the days that passed since I wandered fraying
    tourniquets
& angel stitched
.......I watched the rivers burn
& danced in the alchemy of backwards reveries
........... fairytale
fractured.

**In The Garden Of Orchids**
Under whisperings of my heart
I lay in the hope of love
The imprint of him still carving up my thighs

In breathless whispers
fingers tracing shadows on the outline of my hips

Back arched against his chest
His breath burning reveries down my spine
as he kissed me again
& always
for the first time

## Anatomy of an Indigo – Jackson Browne

These Days
I've been out walking
I don't do much talking these days
These days

These days I seem to think a lot
About the things I forgot to do
And all the times I had a chance to

I've stopped my rambling
I don't do too much gambling these days
These days

These days I seem to think about
How all the changes came about my way
And I wonder if I'll see another highway

I'll keep on moving
I'm bound to be improving these days
These days
And if I seem to be afraid to live the life
That I have made and sown
It's just that I've been healing so long

I've stopped my dreaming
I don't do much dreaming these days
These days
These days I sit on cornerstones
And count the time in quarter tones to ten
Please don't confront me with my failures
I've not forgotten them.

This song was written by Jackson Browne when he was only 16 years old. Does this appear to the thoughts of a normal 16 year old? The depth of introspection and self reflection is remarkable considering his age at the time. "A sense of understanding life and wisdom that is years beyond his worldly years. People within the music business at the time this song was written said this about Browne, "Wise beyond his years" A very fair assessment. This is indicative of an

Indigo. A classic characteristic of Indigos.

Another aspect of Browne's Indigo-ness is this comment that he made in the liner notes on the CD, "Love is Strange "Browne wrote", "It was a flash, as we sometimes used to say in California. A flash in time that went by so effortlessly, and with such pleasure, that I must ask myself if it really happen. "

Another clue is from his 1996 release of "Looking East. " He addressed various aspects of personal growth and social struggle, and their interconnectedness in the world around him. In these thoughts one can see how he was coping with trying to make sense of the world. How he seem to get the big picture and wonder why others don't see it too. He noticed that he has this connection to the world, to nature. He also noticed that for the most part, people were unaware of this interconnectedness. He felt the pain of the abuse that mankind was inflicting on the planet.

This is one of Browns most interesting Indigo characteristics, his legacy as an advocate for social and environmental justice. To quote the Occidental College in Los Angeles, whom in 2004 awarded Browne with a honorary Doctorate of Music, "A remarkable musical career that has successfully combined an intensely personal artistry with a broader vision of social justice. " Again, a classic Indigo characteristic."

Jackson Browne's political views came about and to the public stage shortly after the Three Mile Island accident in March 1979. Browne joined with several other musicians to form the anti-nuclear organization, Musicians United for Safe Energy, also known as MUSE. He became more involved in expressing his political views with the release of his 1986 album, "Lives in the Balance" This album shows his condemnation towards the injustice of the US Policy in Central America. Here are the lyrics to the title tract of Lives in the Balance. In these words, the depth of his pain and concern over the welfare of people he has never met is shown. You can see and hear his anger, compassion and the need to engage his fellow man in becoming aware of the situation. An excellent example of an Indigo knowing of the interconnectedness of the world. This illustrates the empathic nature of an Indigo.

## Lives in the Balance

*I've been waiting for something to happen*
*For a week or a month or a year*
*With the blood in the ink of the headlines*
*And the sound of the crowd in my ear*
*You might ask what it takes to remember*
*When you know that you've seen it before*
*Where a government lies to a people*
*And a country is drifting to war*

*And there's a shadow on the faces*
*Of the men who send the guns*
*To the wars that are fought in places*
*Where their business interest runs*
*On the radio talk shows and the T.V.*
*You hear one thing again and again*
*How the U.S.A. stands for freedom*
*And we come to the aid of a friend*
*But who are the ones that we call our friends*
*These governments killing their own?*
*Or the people who finally can't take any more*
*And they pick up a gun or a brick or a stone*
*There are lives in the balance*
*There are people under fire*
*There are children at the cannons*
*And there is blood on the wire*

*There's a shadow on the faces*
*Of the men who fan the flames*
*Of the wars that are fought in places*
*Where we can't even say the names*
*They sell us the President the same way*

*They sell us our clothes and our cars*
*They sell us everything from youth to religion*
*The same time they sell us our wars*
*I want to know who the men in the shadows are*
*I want to hear somebody asking them why*
*They can be counted on to tell us who our enemies are*
*But they're never the ones to fight or to die*
*And there are lives in the balance*
*There are people under fire*
*There are children at the cannons*
*And there is blood on the wire.*

As you read the lyrics, you can see why so many used this song as a battle cry against America's involvement in Central America. Bill Moyers did a PBS documentary in 1987, The Secret Government: The Constitution in Crisis. This song served as the overall theme and backdrop to the documentary. The action of this one man through a song touch many souls in bringing awareness to a problem that was affecting so many people in the world. This my friend is what being an Indigo is about.

Jackson Browne is considered a forerunner among environmental activists for his concern about planet earth. In 2002, he was awarded the John Steinbeck Award, given to artist whose works exemplify the environmental and social valves that were essential to the great California born author. How uncanny, an award named after an Indigo being given to an Indigo.

And being an Indigo, Browne's personal life has been beset with tragedy. His first wife, Phyllis Major, committed suicide in March of 1976. They had been married less than a year at the time. They had a son, Ethan Zane, born in 1973. Later Browne married Lynne Sweeney, an Australian model, in January 1981. They had one son, Ryan Daniel, born in 1982. This marriage ended in divorce. His relationship with girlfriend, Daryl Hannah ended in a painful breakup in 1992 that was made public. Since that time, Browne has been with long time partner, Diana Cohen, never marrying again.

Jackson Browne's music and bringing awareness to the planet has touched the hearts and souls for over 40 years. His actions, the actions of one man, have brought several changes to so many. In this short bio, you can see several traits of being an Indigo and how just one Indigo can make a difference in the world. For more on Jackson Browne, I encourage you to check out his web site.

# Chapter Five

## What Indigos need to know
## The Keys of being an Indigo that you must know

### 1- Indigos and Ego -

**YOU ARE NOT YOUR EGO** - Within each and every one of us is an inherent deep knowing of who we really are and what we are here to experience and contribute. What keeps this knowing hidden and kept as a mystery is of our own doing. We choose to be blind to it. This is due, in part, to the preconditioning, and it is also partly due to our Ego. It is our Ego that is unwilling to let us see the truth, because the Ego knows that when you realize the truth, its power will be diminished. Now is the time to begin listening to your heart and soul over your mind. Start to focus on your inner voice, rebuild the connection to your inner essence. As an Indigo, know that you are not your Ego, strive to keep it in check while you develop your gifts.

Another way to look at your Ego is this. Imagine that you are an Actor playing a role. Now imagine that the stage is this cosmic universe and you are the Actor. The Ego is merely the role that you are playing, it's not the real you. Your Ego is nothing more than a character being played out.

This is where the break down begins. To show you how silly this Ego issue is let us look to Clint Eastwood. What would everyone think that after Eastwood did the Dirty Harry Movie's, he began to believe he really was Harry Callahan? And as such, Clint Eastwood, thinking that he is Harry Callahan started to roam the streets killing bad guys. Well, I'll tell you, we would lock him up and throw away the key. No doubt about it, he would be locked up.

It is no different with you. You are playing a role in this "movie" of life. This is where your Ego gets involved. The Ego knows that you are fooled by this illusion called life and believe that the Ego is really who you are. This is why the Ego is your worst enemy. The Ego does not want to lose that power. As soon as you realize this one law, you'll be on the road to self discovery and peace. Learn to balance the true self with the Ego, keep the Ego in check. In realizing this truth, you will see that you are not your Ego; your Ego is just a part of you.

Here is another view on Ego from Victor Trucker. He is the Certified Professional Life Coach that is mentioned earlier in the Indigo Children. These are his thoughts on Ego and I agree with him.

"When I use the words "Spiritual Coaching" and "Spiritual Awakening" I am not referring to the imposition of a religious dogma, I am talking about a personal sense of self discovery - the discovery of the Authentic Identity. Most of us live in a false identity (I don't mean a fake name and address); we live in an ego identity, an identity that dies with the body, so it's only *hurrah* is during the seeming life span, where the Spiritual Authentic Self is eternal. By Spiritual Awakening, I mean the process by which we reclaim our lives from the self serving ego identity and return it to our Authentic Identity - that presence that is back of our experienced being-ness. Through identifying with the ego identity we have moved from being powerful creators to being passive observers or perceivers. By shifting away from the attachment to the ego identity and back to our Authentic Self we come into direct contact with our true intent and motives, and the continuous stream of information that life is sending us begins to make perfect sense. We begin to see ourselves, rather than as a tiny speck delineated against the backdrop of infinity, but as being the Perfect Oneness that *IS* Infinity. This clarity flows into every other aspect of our lives and resistance just seems to fall away, conflict and stress become distant memories of what we call the past.

In most cases barriers and blocks that we have carried our entire life (or at least most of it) will simply vanish as if by magic. It is the ego identity that keeps these barriers and blocks in place. The ego clings to them and defines part of itself through them - MY difficult childhood, MY traumatic experiences, MY short-comings, MY lack of education - the list can go on and on and on. Once freed from the ego identity you realize that none of these situations, circumstances or events, none of these "things" defines who you really are. They do not even begin to express your Authentic Self. You are no-'thing', and these are all irrelevant except for the degree to which you attach to them, and allow them the power to own you and control your life. With effective coaching you are able to transcend all of these seemingly insurmountable obstacles and breeze through them like the house of cards that they really are. They are simply a part of a belief structure that you have agreed to, and through this agreement, have learned to accept lies about yourself as truths. As I have stated before - You are absolutely perfect and completely whole and fully innocent right HERE, right NOW. You always have been and always will be, for what you truly are cannot be threatened or diminished in any way."

**Ego, The Greatest Con ever Played** - I have another point I want to make using a movie. I am not going to go into too much detail about the movie but I do want you to see it. I am going to cover the message with you that I took away from it. The movie "Revolver "came out in 2005 and was done by Guy Ritchie. Starring Jason Statham who plays Jake, Ray Liotta plays Dorothy Macha, Andre Benjamin plays Avi, and Vince Pastore plays Zach. I had to see this movie at least a half a dozen times before it made sense to me. Guy Ritchie made this movie to express his beliefs on Kabbalah. Hidden in the movie are mystic Kabbalic ideas, symbolism, and numerology. But I want to focus on the aspect of the Ego which plays the main role in the movie. This is an esoteric movie about the Ego. The plot is disguise as a gangster movie. The story is much deeper than that. It centers on a revenge-seeking con man, Jake that did 7 years in prison on a set up. His weapon is a universal formula that he learned in prison that guarantees victory to its user.  His purpose once out of prison is to destroy Dorothy, the man that put him there. Here is the universal that Jake learned in prison.

1- In every game and con there is always a victim and there is always an opponent. It's good to know when you are the former so you can become the latter.
2- You only get smarter by playing a smarter opponent.
3- The smarter the game the smarter the opponent.
4- Checkers is an example of such a game. Chess is a better example. Debate is even better still.
5- The question is when does the game stop? What is the smartest game one can play?
6- The smartest game? The one that you play on yourself.

Notice that the smartest game that can be played is to play the game on yourself. In the movie Avi is trying to get across this point to Jake.  He tells Jake that the greatest con that the ego ever pulled was making you believe that he *{the ego}* is you. This is the ultimate con, in that no one wants to disconnect from their ego.  Man cannot because of his inability to challenge his lifelong investment into the ego. Life is like a chess board in a metaphoric sense. Jake steps off the chess board by making a conscious effort to turn back everything his ego tells him to do. In doing this, the realization that the mind is nothing more than a tool. This seems to be the point. The problem is when we think of the mind as more than a tool and in fact begin to identify with it. It is in this identity that the ego exists. That is the illusion. This is seen to be the truest and most fundamental application of the Universal Formula. When Jake faces his ego in the elevator he realizes that his own identity is different from his ego. At this moment be becomes free from the bondage of ego and becomes enlighten. Jake ultimately rejects the ego's rules and becomes the opponent instead of the victim.

When we realize and can identify with the ego, that is when we can begin to take the role of the opponent in the con game of life verses the role of the victim. The ego should not define who we are; it is just a tool, a part of the mind. By playing the role of the victim, we give ego control over ourselves. When we take charge by knowing the real identity of who we really are, then at that time we can put the ego in its place. Once in control, we can take charge of our destiny.

When thoughts take over your attention and dominate your mind, you are already identifying with these thoughts or the voice {ego} in your mind. At this point, the thoughts are becoming invested into a sense of self or ego. It is this ego made by your mind that feels the negative and un-empowering emotions creating fear. It grows off these feelings and takes hold and control over you, making you feel incomplete and wanting. When you recognize that this voice {ego} that never stops in your mind pretending to be you, you'll begin to awaken to it and become aware. When you can observe the voice {ego} from the role of the true you, the observer and look upon the voice {ego}, at that time, you are free from the ego. It is a masterly of living in a dualistic world, to know yourself in the awareness that you are not your ego.

## 2- Take Responsibility of your Life -

*"The price of greatness is responsibility"*
*—Winston Churchill*

*"Taking Responsibility. An excerpt from "The Power of Discipline"*                                             *—by Brian Tracy*

*"Your ability and willingness to discipline yourself to accept personal responsibility for your life is essential to happiness, health, success, achievement and personal leadership. Accepting responsibility is one of the hardest of all disciplines, but without it, success is impossible."*

*"The failure to accept responsibility and the attempt to foist responsibility onto others has dire consequences. It completely distorts cause and effect, undermines our character, weakens our resolve, and diminishes our humanity."*

*"When I was twenty-one, I was living in a tiny apartment and working as a construction laborer. I had to get up at 5 a.m. so I could take three buses to work to be there on time. I didn't get home until 7 p.m., usually exhausted. I was making just enough money to get by, with no car, almost no savings, and just enough clothing for my needs. I had no radio or television. In the evenings, if I had enough energy, I would sit in my small apartment at my little table in my kitchen nook and read."*

*"It was the middle of a cold winter, with the temperature at 35 degrees below Fahrenheit. One evening, sitting there by myself at the table, it suddenly dawned on me that, "This is my life."It was like a flashbulb going off in front of my face. I looked at myself and my small apartment, and considered the fact that I had not graduated from high school. The only work I was qualified to do was menial jobs. I earned enough money to pay my basic expenses, but little more. I had very little left over at the end of the month."*

*"It suddenly dawned on me that unless I changed, nothing else was going to change. No one else was going to do it for me. In reality, no one cared. I realized at that moment I was completely responsible for my life, and for everything that happened to me, from that day forward. I was responsible."*

*"I could no longer blame my situation on my difficult childhood, or mistakes that I had made in the past. I was in charge. I was in the driver's seat. This was my life, and if I didn't do something to change it, it would go on like this indefinitely, by the simple process of inertia."*

*"This revelation changed my life. I was never the same again. From that moment forward, I accepted more and more responsibility for everything."* —Brian Tracy

**Taking Responsibility** - First and foremost in life whether you are an Indigo or not is this one law that you must understand and know. One must grasp the power of responsibility in order to move forward. There are at the most basic root of man, three groups of people when dealing with responsibility. See if you recognize anyone in these descriptions

**Living in Denial** - The first group looks at their circumstances and situations and chooses to ignore them. They live in denial and hope that whatever is happening will just go away. As long as these people live life in this state of denial, their lives will not change for the better. Not until they choose to change the way they see life will there be any hope of a better life. This state of thinking reminds me of the Knight of Neet, who kept the belief that it was only a flesh wound while he bleeds to death from having his arms and legs chopped off in battle. This is the common fate of people living in this state. It is just too simple and easy to ignore the truth and live in denial. They let their conditions rule their life. In denial is the absence of responsibility.

**Playing the Victim** - The second group doesn't live in denial. Their fate is worst. They choose to blame everybody and everything for their misfortunes. These people are easy to spot. They are the ones that have an excuse for everything. From being late to work, to not being able to get ahead or living a life of lack, it is always someone else's fault. You can see these people everywhere; they are the ones that have a book of excuses. Let's begin with a few, I didn't go to the right schools, I didn't go to school. I was born poor, it was my parents fault, nobody told me, how was I supposed to know, and the list goes on and on. Always playing the victim, that is their banner, the victim. In this state, we can safely guarantee that they will not get very far in life. In being the victim, they have given control of their condition to others. Their life will always be in lack until they choose to accept responsibility.

**Taking Charge** - The third group are the ones that *Do* take responsibility for their actions, circumstances and situations. This group recognizes the power of accountability. They know they have a choice and they choose to be responsible and take charge of the situation. They don't waste time in denial or blaming others. Instead they spend their energy looking for solutions to fix the problems.

They know that no good will comes out of playing the blame game. The only benefit of blaming others is to create a state of negativity. They choose to be above that and start on the path of solution. Within this decision of being responsibility is the framework for transformation to take place.

**The Three Steps** - This is the crux of my point in three steps.

**One** - When you take Responsibility of a circumstance, you *Own* it.
**Two** - If you own it, then you Control it
**Three** - If you control it, then you can Change it!

---

It is that simple. If don't learn anything else from this book, please just learn this one principle. This simple shift in anyone's thinking can cause significant change to come about in their life. You can either accept responsibility for your life or not. In accepting responsibility, you take ownership of your life and take control of it. In that control is the power to change it. And for those who choose not to, then their life will never change.

**Taking Ownership** - Make today the day that you take ownership of your life. Make decisions to set yourself on the right path. Have the courage to go after your dreams. This is the time to integrate and recover from the changes you've recently experienced. Making the right decisions will give you greater clarity. Today could be the day that brings you greater awareness. This will create a revealing insight that will help you understand the people around you and what has happened to you.

Know that you are not your past nor are you your circumstances. What you are today is nothing more than the results of the decisions that you have made in the past. There is no right or wrong, only results. To get better results, make better decisions.

By taking ownership of your life, you are taking responsibility. In that responsibility is control. Now that you have control over your life, there is no need for worry or doubt. Because when you control your life, you can change it. Having control is having control. Replace doubt with knowing.

All of this can be yours in a blink of an eye. All it takes is for you to make the decision to take control of your life. This simple shift in thinking will bring the instant empowerment. Seize the power that you have within. It's there waiting for you to realize it. Make today the day you decide to live the life you're meant to have.

When you become empowered with the inner strength of your essence, you'll discover how much more life becomes synchronized in achieving your desires and dreams. You'll be able to live more in your imagination. It is within this state that the seeds of manifestation begin to grow. Everything in this world today started out as a thought in someone's imagination. That someone was a person that owned their life because they were responsible; they had ownership of their life.

## 3 - Change your Thoughts, Change your Life -

**Change your thoughts, Change your life** - The fastest way to change your life is to change how you see it. That is the secret. You can't change the external world. It has been this way for centuries. But you can change is how you wish to see the world. Even you can't change your circumstances now you can change how you see it.

Just the mere act of having a shift in your perception can give an immediate change. No matter how distressed your life might be at the moment, you are not your circumstances nor or you your past. No matter how bad it might seem, there is always an opportunity to shift the focus to a more positive one. Know this; you are not your circumstances.

**Victor Frankl's Story** - Victor Frankl was a young doctor in Vienna in 1942 when he and his family were arrested by the Nazis for being Jews. He ended up in Auschwitz, the worst of the concentration camps during World War 2. Going into the camps, the Jews were stripped of everything they own. Everything was taken from them, their clothing, pictures, personal belongings, even their names. The Germans replaced their names with numbers. Victor Frankl's number was  119,104. During this time Victor Frankl came up with this belief,

*"Everything can be taken from a man but one thing; the last of the human freedoms - to choose one's attitude in any given set of circumstances, to choose one's own way."*

There he chose to look for the goodness in the most horrible place imaginable. When others refuse to eat the soup because of a rotting fish head floating in the pot, Victor Frankl gave thanks for the meager meal that would keep him alive for another day. He felt blessed to see the sunrise every morning. He chose to keep faith and hope that he would survive this ordeal. He discovered that those who held a vision of the future, a bright future, one of freedom and being reunited with family , even with the task of surviving being near hopeless, were more likely to endure  the suffering and survive.

In 1946 Victor Frankl wrote a book titled, " Man's Search for Meaning." describing the trials and tribulations of the years spent in the concentration camps. Out of this ordeal came a book so profound that even today, by some, it is considered to be one of the most influential books in the United States. The book has been translated into 24 different languages and has sold over 10 million copies worldwide. We can all learn a great deal from this man. I would recommend to everyone to read his book, "Man's Search for Meaning."

Here are just a few of the thoughts that Victor Frankl kept in mind during these days of a hell on earth,

"The salvation of man is through love and in love.  I understood how a man who has nothing left in this world still may know bliss, be it only for a brief moment, in the contemplation of his beloved."

*"A thought transfixed me: for the first time in my life l saw the truth as it is set into song by so many poets, proclaimed as the final wisdom by so many thinkers. The truth—that love is the ultimate and the highest goal to*

*which man can aspire. Then I grasped the meaning of the greatest secret that human poetry and human thought and belief have to impart: The salvation of man is through love and in love. I understood how a man who has nothing left in this world still may know bliss, be it only for a brief moment, in the contemplation of his beloved. In a position of utter desolation, when man cannot express himself in positive action, when his only achievement may consist in enduring his sufferings in the right way—an honorable way—in such a position man can, through loving contemplation of the image he carries of his beloved, achieve fulfillment. For the first time in my life I was able to understand the meaning of the words, 'The angels are lost in perpetual contemplation of an infinite glory."*

If Victor Frankl could master such a profound state of thought through just changing the way he decided to view the world, then this power can belong to anyone that so desires it. There are no excuses for anyone to be in a state of depression, despair, agony, or any other limiting emotions. Let Victor Frankl be your role model in empowering you to take charge and change your life in an instance!

## 4 - The Eleven Emotions Indigos should avoid -

These disempowering emotions apply to everyone, not just Indigos. But these do seem to affect Indigos more than the average person. It is important to be aware of these peace stealing emotions and learn to guard against them, and if they do seek up on you, how to deal with them. Here is the list.

1-Anger- to cause harm, retaliation, furious, maddened, irate
2-Fear-horror, terror, dismay, panic, dread, anxiety, apprehension
3-Lost- dazed, wasted, astray, used, confused, destroyed, bewildered
4-Guilt- sin, blame, misstep, fault,

5-Grief- misery, sadness, affliction, heartache, woe, anguish, sorrow

6-Jealousy- suspicion, envy, greed, covetousness, resentful ness

7-Insecurity- uneasy, nervous, uncertain, shaky

8-Inferiority- lower, poorer, secondary, mediocre

9-Despair- depression, hopelessness, gloom, desperation, pessimism

10-Distrust- unbelief, suspect, doubt, hesitation, mistrust

11-Loneliness-solitude, isolation, seclusion, alienation, des olated, deserted

There are more that we can add to the list but in truth, most are variations of these negative emotions listed here. At the signs of any of these peace robbing emotions starting to creep up, it is essentially imperative to rid yourself of them immediately. One way to train yourself in ridding yourself of them is to understand how they come to be. There is no real anger or fear in the world. It is only our interpretation of these emotions based on our experiences that make them what they are. Lets look how the experiences come into play. Our experiences fall into a dualistic pattern. We talked about this briefly in an earlier chapter. It is this dualistic pattern, dualistic world that we live in that divides the world into the experience and what is experienced. Now imagine that you are the "I" or the observer in this and the experience is the "subject" or the object. While we are having an experience the "I" starts to consider and think about the what is being experienced, the "subject" Here is the breakdown, the thoughts are only reflections of the experiences. The experience is what it is. It just is! It is the "I", the observer that defines the experience. No matter how one reflects on and thinks about the experience, it is impossible to become the experience. You cannot make the experience your own. The experience has its own existence.

Let us put in another way. Two people are sharing lunch. While the two are together in the same time space and place sharing the same meal. No matter if both are eating the same meal from the same plate. The experience is the lunch itself. That is an identity in itself. The lunch is "just is" it doesn't matter what anyone thinks about the lunch.

Within the lunch, the lunch is just is. It is the interpretation by the observers that decide on how the experience will be defined. No matter how similar the two people are, their experiences of the lunch will be different. All one can do is reflect on the experience but can't become the experience. That is the curse of the dualistic world. This is where the separation comes into play in this 3 dimensional world.

So how does this play into the pitfalls of negative emotions. Simple, choose on how you interpret the experience. You are the observer and have the right to choose how you want to reflect on the experience. The experience is only an object. It has no meaning. It is you that gives the meaning to it.

**Meanings** - To give you another example of the meanings placed on experiences or in this case objects. Let's take a hundred dollar bill. Let's take it to the zoo and throw this hundred dollar bill into the gorilla cage. What are the gorillas going to do? Nothing because the gorilla has no perspective or meaning associated with the hundred dollar bill. To him, it is nothing and he treats it as such. Now throw the same hundred dollar bill into a crowd. Now, what do you get? You get chaos from the people fighting to get that hundred dollar bill. Why, because they have put a meaning and an association to the hundred dollar bill. That is the difference and the key. Any experience, whether it is eating lunch with a friend, watching a movie or having a tough day at work. It only matters as much as the meaning that is attached to it. You do not have to let the experience dictate to you, it is you that dictates the experience.

**Puppet verses the Puppet Master** - What happens when you do lose it and let anger take over? The way I like to answer this question is as follows. When you allow someone to get under your skin and let them get you angry, what you have done is give control over yourself to that person. In essence, you have become a puppet and given the other person the strings to pull you into whatever direction they choose to drag you in. The most logical thing to do is to cut the strings and take control back. Why would you let someone else have control over you? The only way anyone can have control over you is if you decide to give them that power. But here is the problem. For the most part, people believe that their life is based on external forces. That is wrong! You control how you decide to experience the experience. You have the power to interpret how you want the event to affect you. Remember, you are the Puppet Master, not the Puppet.

I know this is a daily struggle, trying to maintain control over your emotions and letting someone get to you. It takes practice and you will need to find a way to get back to center when you sense that you are losing your cool. One of the ways I get back to center is to remember the words of Rene Descartes,

*"Whenever anyone has offended me, I try to raise my soul so high that the offense cannot reach it."*

No matter how much you may advance on your path, this is one distraction that you will have along the way. So, find a way to deal with it, and at the first signs of one of these negative emotions creeping in, get out the scissors, cut the strings and regain the Master of your domain.

**Preconditioning** - All of this goes back to your preconditioning. It is a must that you reprogram yourself off the limiting disempowering precepts that is holding you back. You have been preconditioned to believe the image in the mirror is real, that is the illusion. Imagine yourself looking at your reflection in a mirror. You notice that you don't like the way your hair looks so you try to comb the hair in the mirror. Sounds crazy doesn't it? But is exactly what most people do. This is the secret; all change begins within you, not outwardly. When someone gets you off balance and you look to them to get rebalanced, then you have tried to comb the hair in the mirror. Don't look into the mirror for change, look within. You have the power to create your own illusion in the mirror by changing your sense of reality by how you interpret the world. Manifesting your reality is that simple. Take control of your life today!

Once you discover this secret, you'll be free from these negative emotions. Make a conscious decision to control how you choose your experiences. Take a lesson from Victor Frankl and the others mentioned in this book and realize that the world is what it is but you control how you choose to see it.

**Loneliness** - This is an area that deserves special attention. This is from a letter I received from an Indigo and I want to share it with you to show how loneliness plays on the soul.

*"Is anyone feeling lost, lonely and confused? Every day I fight to remain positive and every day I look for the beauty in the world and yet I feel so disconnected and the yearning for home is sometimes overwhelming. It's the unspoken truth that I carry within my heart from day to day, and what keeps me grounded is my knowledge that I chose to be here for a purpose, but sometimes it eluded me and my path seems shrouded in a veil of confusion. I have spent most of my life medicated, either with drugs or alcohol and for the first time I been sober for 3 weeks straight. Tonight I struggle within myself because it is easier to feel nothing than it is to feel everything. Can anyone relate?"*

One common thread among Indigos at one time or another is a sense of loneliness. As you can see this young woman has had her share of dealing with loneliness. I am going to show you that in some ways, loneliness is trying to communicate with you. There are several reasons you can feel lonely. At times it is to serve as a signal to get you to realize that there is a disconnection between where you are now and where you should be. At these times, you need to revaluate where you are with all aspects of life. These feelings can rise from being around people that are draining your energy. If this is the case, it is imperative to remove yourself from these low energy people as soon as possible.

It doesn't matter if it is in a family setting, work or friends. Get some distance from them and their low energy fields. You don't have to necessarily have to pack up and leave but you do need to get some separation between you and them. Place these people outside the range of your energy field. You know that Indigos do not fare well dealing with drama. It is normal to feel lonely around people that don't understand or get you. It is their inability to feel at the depths that you do that creates the disconnection. It is your essence that is sensitive to their uncaring that creates the feeling of loneliness. Look to replace these people with others more like you to keep you grounded and centered.

Another signal that loneliness can mean is that you are off the path. Loneliness comes when there is an absence of love, connection, purpose and feeling of belonging. Loneliness is serving as an indicator that you are unhappy with your current path and you need to revaluate if you should be on another path. Remember at these times that loneliness is merely a reminder that you need to find your place in life.

Everyone at time or another will feel loneliness, this is natural. But, remember at times solitude serves as an integral part in getting to know yourself. Being lonely is a state of mind and a perspective that you should study and learn from. It is nothing more than your subconscious asking you to take time for an introspective review of what you need to do to get back on the path.

**The Power of Forgiveness, Compassion and Love** - In order to combat negative emotions, you'll need the proper defense. The paradox to this is in order to defeat these negative emotions, you must surrender to them, to let go of holding on to them. This is done through forgiveness and compassion. When Jesus gave the Sermon on the Mount he said,

*"But I say unto you, Love your enemies, bless them that curse you, do good to them that hate you, and pray for them which despitefully use you and persecute you"*
—*Matthew 5:43-44*

Whatever you think, feel and send out into the world, the same will come back to you. You cannot send out harm without harm coming back to you. The same is true with love. As you send love out to the world, love will come back. This is the meaning of the words of Jesus. If you go for tick for tack, you'll receive the like in return. Dealing in negative energies will only bring more negative energies back to you. It is through the acts of forgiveness and compassion that will foster love and raise you above the fray of these lower energies. No matter what comes your way, remember people like Victor Frankl and his ordeals. It is in how you decide to view the circumstances and interpret them. Choose a higher path and rise above. Live a life with appreciation and compassion for whatever comes across your path. Have a sense of gratitude for all in life. Give the gift of love to all adversity. Become non-judgmental, have respect for all living creatures and beings. Build a fortress with these elements and no type of negative energy or person will be able to penetrate the walls. Treat forgiveness, compassion and love like a candle. In the darkest of rooms, in the darkest of nights, the light of the smallest candle will repeal the darkness. But the all the darkness in the universe can put out the light of that small candle. This is true with love. This is the power of these positive higher vibrating emotions over the negative energies of life. Take the words of Jesus to heart and keep them in your thoughts on a daily basis. Practice and put into use these words and you'll see a difference in your life. Live with forgiveness, compassion and love!

## 5. Improve your Environment, Improve your Life -

This is an important principle to understand. Change your thoughts, change your life. Improve your environment, improve your life. It doesn't matter where you are at this point in your life. It doesn't matter! You can make the decision now to improve your life. All it takes is the desire to get up and do something about it. You are not your circumstances; there are no excuses that apply to you. Whatever your current situation is, it is only the results of previous decisions that you have made. Make it a point today to get better results from now on. And it can start now by improving your environment.

If you want to live an inspiring life, then create an inspiring environment. Surround yourself with the things that inspire you. You will assimilate to whatever environment you are in. So this is important to understand. Decide that you are ready to live the life you deserve. Make the changes that you know are needed. If money is an issue, then listen to inspirational music on the radio. Be careful what you choose to watch on TV, watch inspirational movies. Go to the museums and look at inspirational artwork. Do whatever it takes to surround yourself with the best that you can. Remember this law; you will become a reflection of your environment, a reflection of your mind. Be very mindful of controlling your environment. Create the state of mind that brings you peace, happiness and joy through your surroundings. This is critical to understand and practice. Environment is important.

Your environment includes your home, car, job, relationships, friends and your surroundings. Don't become overwhelm by how large or seemly impossible situation that you may be in. It all begins with taking small steps. Let's take a look at what you can do with your home, car and job. Start with your home. Practice bringing greatness into everything you do. Clean up your home. If it isn't organize then organize it. Start with the closets and work your way through the entire home. Put everything in its place. Let your home become an extension of your inner greatness. Let the pride of who and what you are shine in the outwardly appearances of your home. Do the same with your car. If your car is dirty then clean it, if there is trash in the back seat, then clean it out. Let your car become an extension be an extension of your inner greatness. It is the same with your job. If there are areas that you can improve on, then improve on them. If your desk is a mess, then straighten it up. Get it organize. Whatever you do for a job, insure that you are doing your best and that your greatness is showing through your work. Let your work be an extension of your inner greatness.

There is nothing you can do today about the results of your actions of the past. But you do have control of the results that you want to see in the future by how you treat today. Decide to take the steps today to insure the results you want to see.

All you really have is today, now. That's it, just today. That is all you can really control. So act now, take charge of doing what needs to be done. You can't deal with where you are not nor can to deal with is yet to be, but you can deal with this moment.

Start with doing great things in a small way and notice the changes. As you begin to see the improvements you'll be more motivated to do even more. This is the key to this principle, start with becoming great within and start the change outwardly. Start with small steps and grow on that. Remember there is nothing too small or too insignificant that you can afford to overlook. Know that you can expect magnificent results from the smallest of acts. There is no way of knowing the outcome of anything we do. Treat every detail with the greatest consideration as to insure the outcome you want. Do not assume something trivial doesn't matter, everything matters.

On relationships, did you know that is said that 80% of life's satisfaction comes from meaningful relationships? The same principle for you actions in your home, car and job applies to your relationships too? To improve your relationships with love ones and friends practice showing your greatness in your actions. If your relationship is meaningful to you and seems meant to be then it would stand to reason that you would want the best out of it. The funny thing about this principle is when you take the responsibility in improving your relationship; the other person in the relationship will more than likely choose to take responsibility too without them being aware of it.

Here are a few steps you can use to improve your relationships. Apply these principles to see results immediately and get the most out of your relationships. Make the decision to make it work. Make a commitment to do whatever it takes. Practice respect and kindness towards your partner. It doesn't matter if they have earn it or not, give them respect, kindness, love, and compassion. Give these gifts to your partner without expecting anything in return. Give from your heart with the knowing that you don't need any acknowledgement. Do not allow your partner to affect you in a negative manner. Practice tolerance, patience and acceptance. Be determined and persistent in following through with your kindness. Since you know the outcome, it should be easy to stay the path. Often times, so many people give up too soon. If they had just stayed the course a little longer they would have succeed. Be true to yourself; let your actions speak of your inner greatness. Give because you desire to give, not to receive something in return.

## 6. Own your Failures -

This may seem like an ill-advised statement to make but follow the logic and you'll see how owning your failures can make a significant difference in your life. We all deal with failures, it is part of life. They cannot be avoided and must be faced. It is in the failures that we learn and grow. But that doesn't make going through failures any less painful. Let's take a different approach to the age old issue of dealing with failures. See how a simple shift in perspective can create a new empowering view towards failure.

Suppose I told you that I can guarantee you that you will fail 90% of the time. I can guarantee you that! 90% of the time, you will fail. How would you react to that deal? Before jumping to the obvious answer give me a moment.

It is a given that we are going to fail in every aspect of life, relationships and business. That we know. Look at Baseball. If a batter has a batting average of 330 he is considered a great hitter. In hitting 330 the batter will have failed the other 670 times. In baseball, failing 2/3rds of the time still makes you a success. Failures are a part of life. It's in how you decide to look at it. So, let's get back to that guarantee.

In the guarantee of failing 90% of the time there is the guarantee that you will succeed the other 10% of the time. That is the secret; it is in the guarantee of that 10% of succeeding that we need to focus on. We do not see the success of the 10%. Instead we focus on the 90% of failures. Because it is the fear of rejection from the failures that holds us back from taking risk to improve our lives, whether in business or our personal lives. We must learn to endure the failures in order to succeed. The key is creating the shift in thinking to overcome the rejection of failure.

Let's look at the guarantee a little closer. Let's say you are in sales. You have a guarantee that every tenth call you make will be a winner, imagine that, every tenth call will be a winner. How would that affect the way you deal with the other nine calls that don't work out? Well, you should be happy to get those nine calls out of the way as fast as possible. Because you know that as soon as you get those nine calls out of the way, there will be that tenth call that will pay off. A great way to look at it is if your tenth call is worth $500.00 dollars that would make all ten calls worth $50.00 each. Now with that mindset, how would you take the rejection of those nine calls? I would think that I would want to get rejected those nine times in order to get to the tenth call knowing that every call was worth $50.00 each. These simple shifts in thinking will overcome your fear of failures and make the experience more enjoyable.

This is a crass example of this theory. When I was a teenager I had a friend named Larry. He would date every girl who would go out with him. Most times he would go on a date with a girl that frankly, I would never consider taking out, much less being seen with. I know this sounds mean, but remember we were kids at the time. Larry was asked several times by me as well as his other friends why he did this. His answer was a simple one. He said that the law of averages said that one out of every ten girls he dated would be a drop dead gorgeous knock-out. So he was only trying to get the other nine out of the way to get to the tenth one. And I must admit, he did have his share of successful dates with those 10%. I am not suggesting that this is the purpose of this principle or one should follow in Larry's steps in dating but I want to illustrate the mindset that Larry had in approaching the subject of failure. He embraced his 90% because in the end he knew that the 10% would make it more than worthwhile.

While this gets a little more complicated with relationships, the lesson should be in failure there is success. Even if all you learn is what not to do, that is leading you in the right direction. You are not your failures or should you take them too seriously. In failure there is opportunity to learn and grow. Use the opportunities to pick up knowledge and the confidence that your time to succeed is coming. Do not let the failures get you down. They are only stepping stones to the winning finish line. Never consider for a moment that intelligence is a factor. No one is smarter than you. During your trials of enduring the failures work on your knowledge and build your skills. Apply what you have learn learned along the way to increase the percentage of the winning times. Learn to look upon the trying times as a chance to refine yourself and make yourself more capable of handling the success when it arrives. Learn to own your failures and embrace them, they are going to a part of life so might as well make them into an asset.

## 7. Symptoms of Spiritual Awakening for Indigos -

Before getting into the symptoms of spiritual awakening I would like to discuss the reasons the symptoms come about. The causes of these symptoms can be your reluctance to accept the changes that you are going through. It could be that you are in denial of what is happening. It can be because of the preconditioning and group-think that you cannot let go of.

One theory I have is some of these symptoms of spiritual awakening are attribute to your chakras being blocked and not letting the energy to flow. The universe is there and wanting to infused into you the blessings of the divine love of the source. If you are in resistance to this energy, then there will be blockages in the charkas. You can have these resistances and not even be aware of them. It can be something that your logical mind decides to dismiss. The issues with dismissing these feelings are just because you think you dismissed it, doesn't mean it went away. Instead the issue becomes lodged in the sub-conscious creating these blockages.

At times these symptoms are in your sub-conscious and the inner being is trying to communicate with you. You need to take notice and deal with these concerns. Learn to listen to your body and inner voice, they are there and waiting to talk to you. It is in the silence of meditation where you can communicate and work out these issues. Most symptoms are un-resolved issues waiting for you to realize that you need to deal with them. Imagine a river; the water cannot flow if there are obstacles blocking the path of the river.

And if the water can't flow in the manner that it is meant to then a disaster will follow. The way a river flows is not that much different than the way divine energy flows. Symptoms of spiritual awakening are like the river blocked by obstacles. The point is to clear out all the obstacles and negative issues that are preventing the flow of divine energy.

For Indigo's, spiritual awakening is a crisis. Your old belief system is exhausting all possibilities to make sense of this new way of thinking and is resisting change. A new form of consciousness is trying to break through. Before the spiritual awakening can emerge, the old system must be dispose of. A form of mutation is taking place, an internal battle between the old ways and the new you, hence forth the symptoms. Once you are aligned with this new paradigm, the change will be spontaneous. The manifestation of the "spiritual you" will happen suddenly with all the possibilities of the spirit world being present and available to you.

**Symptoms** - When Indigos go through a spiritual awakening or working on attaining the next level, they may experience some of these symptoms. These are a sign that their Indigo-ness is coming out and wanting to be acknowledged and to reconnect to the divine source. Not every Indigo will suffer these symptoms but if you are, let go and go with the flow. It is part of the process that you must go through. With a knowing, at least you will be aware and have an understanding of the changes taken place. The best way to describe it is like being on one heck of a roller-coaster. Buckle up and enjoy the ride. Here are a few of the changes that you might experience.

**Introduction to Chakras** - Chakras are our energy centers. They serve as the openings for our life energy to flow into and through our system and aura. They serve to vitalize the physical body and to bring development of our consciousness. They connect the physical, mental and emotional aspects of our self with the Divine Source.

There are Seven Chakras. Each Chakra vibrates or rotated at a different speed. The first chakra, known as the Root Chakra operates at the lowest speed and the seventh chakra know as the Crown Chakra operates at the fastest speed. Each of the seven chakras are related by their own color. The colors are red, orange, yellow, green, blue, indigo, and violet.

The seven Chakras are located deep within the physical body along the spinal column. Each of the seven chakras are associated with different parts of the body. Each chakra represents a set of desires that relate to a particular element. Understanding these seven chakras helps in balancing your life and to achieve spiritual awakening. Knowing the importance of these chakras are fundamental in attaining higher states of consciousness and for the development of spiritual awareness.

The seven chakras are the Root Chakra, known as the security center, the Sacral Chakra, known as the sensation center, the Solar Plexus Chakra, known as the power center, the Heart Chakra, known as the living love center, the Throat Chakra, known as the cornucopia center, the Third Eye Chakra, known as the consciousness awareness center, and the Crown Chakra, known as the cosmic consciousness center.

When the seven chakra are open and in balance your physical and emotional systems will operate at its' optimal level. When the Chakras are not in balance or blocked, the energy or life force will be slowed down. The symptoms of this blockage can affect the physical and mental health. In a state of blockage, diseases can manifest as well as a host of other negative effects. These symptoms can also affect the thought process. Symptoms include fear, doubt, anxiety, negative thoughts, etc. Any imbalances that exist within any of the chakra may have a profound effect on the physical or mental aspects. Constant balances between all seven chakras are required to keep a state of physical and mental health.

**Chakra Awakening** - Most of these symptoms are due to your Chakras opening up and expanding to receive more energy from the divine source. The symptoms of the activation of these Chakras are experience as an intense increase of activity at the top of your head running down your spine to the lower back. The sensations include feeling a crawling, prickly, itching, and tingling. At times you might feel like you are coming out of your skin. Another sensation is burst of energy running down from the top of the head down the spine, not unlike a sensation of an electrical shock. While scary and frightening, this is nothing to be concern about. Best approach is to just relax and let go and go with the flow. It is the beginning of your chakras opening up. This is necessary in order to open up to receive divine energy and guidance.

**Sleep Patterns** - Another symptom is a radical change in your sleep patterns. You might go from sleeping the normal 7 to 8 hours a night to sleeping 14 to 16 hours to sleeping just a few hours. Sleep patterns can go from sleeping all night to waking up every few hours. You might be sleeping more than usual and still feel tired. Or you may have this sense of energy without hardly any sleep. Just go with the flow and don't fight it. If you are going through periods of being unable to sleep, take that time to meditate. All you can do is ride it out. It is your body adjusting to the new energy and awakening of your chakras.

**Emotions** - This can be a real rollercoaster ride with the sudden changes in your emotions. These symptoms are the result of bringing to the forefront unresolved issues within the mind and soul. These issues must be resolved and dealt with in order for the new system to be implemented. Because of the amount of new energy required with this paradigm shift, old ways need to be dealt with and released. It is the removal of these emotional blocks that will free up the Heart Chakra that will allow the new divine energy to flow through you. Trying to repress or dismiss these symptoms will only create more problems for you. You will adjust and deal with these issues or you will stay in a state of imbalance. The good news is as you get closer to spiritual awakening, it will be easier to deal with and let go of this unnecessary burdens.

You may have severe mood swings. You go from feeling happy to feeling depress with no apparent reason. Deep feelings of depression and loneliness can manifest at any anytime. Along with these symptoms, apprehension and anxiety compound the problems. Unable to relate these issues with others because you yourself don't understand what is happening doesn't help matters either. You may even experience bouts of being angry for no reason, just looking for something or someone to unload on. There may be a sudden urge to cry or intense feelings of guilt or complete lack of enthusiasm.

These emotions are related to your Heart Chakra. You are experiencing these symptoms because the Heart Charka is beginning to open up to take in more energy. The key here is to not let these emotions be directed at anyone or anything. Observe these emotions for what they are. Go inside yourself to accept these emotions. Experience them and feel them, breath deep and be in the moment. Feel them and let them run their course and they will go away. The reason for these emotions is for you to grieve the letting go of the old ways including relationships that are no longer in harmony.

Be gentle with yourself, this cleansing process is necessary to experience the letting go of the old you. Look at it as a death of the material you, knowing that a rebirth is about to take place. Try your best to keep these emotions in check and realize that again, these are your heart chakra awakening.

**Changes in Weight and Eating Habits** - Changes in weight and eating habits are another symptom that can wreak havoc on your system. With the sudden changes in weight, there might be a fear of this weight change being permanent. As long as your body is not asking for anything harmful, give it what it wants, even if it is a food you have never eaten before. These issues in your weight and eating habits are extensions of the fears that have been suppressed are now being dealt with. Being physically hunger or not is just an extension of the inner conflict. Don't worry any changes in your eating habits and the weight, they will return to normal once the body adjusts to the charkas being activated.

One issue during this time that might be noticeable is a sudden like or dislike for certain foods. This is your body realizing what it needs and what it doesn't want. This is a form of your body removing toxins and cleansing itself. The Chakras are integrating and healing unsolved issues.

One point that is necessary is to insure that you have a diet that is optimal to your health. Besides, a healthy diet is a benefit regardless if you are having issues or not. Stay away from harmful foods and drinks; these will only prolong the process. As you become more spiritual, your body will demand a diet more aligned with that spiritually.

**Sensitivity** - You might notice an increased sensitivity to sight, hearing and touch. One symptom is having the ability to see Auras on people, animals and plants. Some objects might appear to be translucent when you know they are solid. The colors might be more vibrant and seem alive.

With this new sight, you'll be able to appreciate the beauty of nature. With practice you'll soon see, hear and be able to touch the purity of the universe and know what is unnatural. Don't be afraid of these changes, rather learn from them.

With foods, you'll be able to taste what is organic and what contain chemicals. You'll have a desire to stay clear of what is unnatural. What was once thought of as being tasty will now taste awful. This is your system gaining insight into the harmonic balance of nature and letting you know.

There is also the symptom of being hypersensitive to vibration. You will be constantly checking your phone thinking that you have it on vibrate as well as feel the vibrations and not knowing the source. When listening to music, you'll notice that along with hearing it, you'll also feel it. It's Okay.

The symptoms of hypersensitive hearing might be so acute that you will swear that you are hearing things. There might be times while laying in bed at night you will hear sounds that no else can hear. One story I was told was of a young man that could hear and tell the difference of the road noise caused by the tires on 18 wheelers on the interstate while in bed at night. The problem was he was several miles from the interstate where the big trucks were running but he could tell a friend via a cell phone who was on the interstate what trucks were running. To the amazement of the friend, the young man was right every time.

Another story is of a young woman claimed that she could hear the buzzing of the bees outside her office windows. When she could see the bees from her window, she would walk up to the see the bees several feet away flying about. At times she said she could close her eyes and to be able to smell the flowers along with hearing the bees. Some Indigos have said to have felt the presence of bees while smelling the fragrance of cut flowers, closing their eyes, they could envision the bee connecting with the flower. This is a wonderful gift. It shows an interconnectedness and attunement to nature. This is one of the most precious gifts of Indigos.

**Spirit Guides** - Some have claimed to have seen and felt spirit guides around them. This is nothing to be afraid of. It is a spiritual awareness of higher dimensions being developed. Some will begin to channel with these spirits. Some will develop this gift through dreams while others will discover it while meditating. It might begin with an inner voice that at first you'll think is your intuitive voice. After awhile, you'll know the difference. If you worried about Evil or Malicious Spirits, just tell yourself that you will not entertain any of these spirits, that they are not welcomed. These symptoms are being brought on by the veil between this world and theirs dissolving as you awaken. While scary at first, don't be afraid or worried, embrace the changes and go on. Remember that these spirits are there to help you on your journey to Spiritual Awakening. Ask for their help and guidance, they're here for you.

I would recommend reading any of the books by Ruth Montgomery. Educate yourself on this subject. This is another wonderful gift of being an Indigo. If you are fortunate enough to have this gift, then you are blessed!

**Health Issues** - Some Indigos have experience so many different health issues and symptoms over a short period of time that they will cause their doctors to scramble for an answer. Some doctors may test them or even diagnose them with MS, Chronic Fatigue Syndrome, or Fibromyalgia. While these are serious issues, other symptoms may be less serious. Some of these may include headaches, back pains, dental issues, and digestive issues, feeling constantly exhausted, muscle spasms, chest pains and heartburn, along with a host of more issues.

One point that I want to make concerns the symptoms of fatigue and feeling exhausted. Keep a journal and make a note of when you have a major break-through or a shift in your awareness. Most times, the after effects of these events will be fatigue and exhaustion. It is your body adjusting to the changes happening to you psychically and spiritually. Take note of these changes so you may recognize them for what they are. No worries just take the necessary steps to rest and recover. Learn to go with the flow; it is all by design with a purpose.

Now do not take a chance with your health. If you think there is an issue with your health, by all means seek medical help with any physical issues. Once it is determine that it is not a medical issue, relax and accept the ride. Don't fight it, it won't do any good. Let go because it is only temporary.

**Mental Issues** - Along with health issues there are mental issues that come into play. The most common of these symptoms are the feeling of dread or the impending sense that something bad is about to happen. The fear of a sense of the unknown, especially one that seems that doom and gloom are around the corner can be frightening.

Memory lost or déjà vu is another issue that is experienced during these times. One example that describes these moments in a humorous way is when you open the refrigerator, not remembering if you open it to take something out or if you just put something in. These moments can be very frustrating.

At times, you'll seem to be unable to talk. You know what you want to say but for some reason, you just can't get the words out. Then there is the sense of sudden burst of energy passing through you, coming with no warning. It is like an electrical shock that will jolt you into action, unnerving you to the core, causing you to question your sanity. With these jolts, you'll experience impatience to a new degree. Even though you know better, you'll still act on these impulses causing more problems. Your life will seem like a yoyo going from not wanting to do anything to wanting to save the world in a flash.

Along with having a sense of feeling completely lost is unsettling to say the least. The sense of lost comes from feelings of not knowing your purpose. The conflict is in the deep desire for knowing the meaning of life, to be spiritually connected and feeling that you are off the path. This comes from realizing that the material world does not hold the answers. While you may feel off-tract, you are where you need to be. The anxiety comes from you wanting to get there as fast as possible but unsure of the way.

All these symptoms are the result of the body and spirit integrating together into the new paradigm. It is a form of the cleansing of the mental aspects of the old you. It is the mind trying to adjust without knowing how or why. While these times can seem overwhelming, it is a natural process that must be endured. This is a re-alignment of your energy getting into balance with your Chakras. It is normal so just go with it.

**Sacred Geometry** - It might be around this time you become aware of Sacred Geometry. You will notice shapes that you might have never notice before. You'll begin to see patterns in shapes and numbers everywhere you look, especially in nature. You will feel a connection to these shapes and probably will not understand why. This is normal.

At around this time, you might begin to see certain numbers over and over. Some claim to see numbers like 11:11. For instance, they wake up at 11:11 or notice the time during the day or see this number on a billboard or street address. Whenever you see the same numbers repeating, whatever the numbers are, like these over and over, it is the universe trying to communicate with you, letting you know that you are getting in sync. It is coming into alignment with the divine universe and seeing the beauty of divine creation in Sacred Geometry. I know several Indigos that connect with the intelligent design of Sacred Geometry and don't even realize it. We will discuss this subject later in the book.

**Disassociation with Linear Time** - You may feel that time is moving rapidly or maybe standing still at times. Keeping up with the days of the week become a chore. It seems that one day runs into the next. This is a good thing. It shows your advancement away from the material world and back into the natural world that you were meant to be in. There is a natural time that is in harmony with the Earth. The calendar that we use is not in harmony or balance. The Mayan knew that the universe has a rhythm and balance to it and live life accordingly. With the introduction of the Gregorian calendar by Pope Gregory XIII on February, 24, 1582, Mankind has been out of sync with nature ever since. Your disassociation with this method of time keeping is a good sign that your authentic self is getting back in balance with the universe.

**Life Changing Events** - One aspect of spiritual awakening is having major life changing events take place in your life. There might be just one event or several, it is different for everyone. This is your Authentic Self either shedding all unnecessary and unneeded aspects of your life or teaching you the lessons you need to learn about life. These events can include death of love ones, loss of material possessions, job loss or major career change, major illness to you or love ones. These are taking place in your life for a reason. It may be to teach you detachment because of your clinging to material things or to show you that you're focusing on the wrong areas of your life. They may be to increase your awareness to needing to be more compassionate and loving. Or maybe you just need to learn to let go.

It is amazing how the universe will get your attention. These events are to be a benefit for you in the long run, even if at the time, they seem more like a nightmare. Sometimes in life, your greatest gifts will come disguise has your worst nightmares. Look for the meaning and the lessons that lie within these events.

**Life Changing Thoughts** - You may have a sudden urge to find "yourself" or to make life changing decisions in an instance. You may suddenly want to sell everything you have because you realize it isn't needed, that there is more to life than carrying around a bunch of stuff. Now, this is a time to take a time out and think things out because this is going to come hard and fast. Stay calm and listen to your heart. There will be this sudden need to find your purpose and get your affairs in order and to streamline your life. This urge will be followed by the need to start living your purpose, even you if are not sure what that purpose is. These feelings can and will be overpowering.

You might feel the need to quit the job in the city and move out to the country. Or go into a new career. You might have a sudden feeling that your life is in chaos and an urgency to get it right. Also, you might have a sudden need for solitude and wanting to spend time in introspection. Also, a feeling of something is about to happen and a need to address this feeling but don't know how. You may have a need to get in touch with nature and connect with spirit. All these feelings and emotions may rain down on you at once. My advice is this, Listen to your heart and soul, not the logical side of your brain. What is happening is your sub conscious is receiving divine knowledge and wanting to act on it.

Listen to your inner voice. If your intuition is telling you to do it, to go for it, then do it, follow your intuition and heart, it is your spirit guiding you. Listen to your inner voice. You will always be lead down the right path when you listen to spirit in the stillness of your mind.

**Dreams** - Dreams, now you want to talk about being completely confused mentally and emotionally. You might have dreams so vivid and real that you will have a hard time in determining which world is the real world. There will be times you will not be able to distinguish between the dream world and the real world. Your memories will be blend into a mesh that you make you think that you are losing your mind. Don't let this scare you. In your pursuit of mystical knowledge you'll discover the ease in being able to enter into lucid dreams. In these dream states, you might receive messages from the Astral World. You might even be able to travel into different Astral Worlds. This is an attempt to advance your education by higher beings. Take notice of the details, hints and messages when in this dream state. Learn to explore these other realms. Don't be afraid to ask questions or ask for guidance. These dream states can be a staging ground for a break-through in

Cosmic Awareness. As your self-awareness intensifies and you master your astral body during these dreams, the possibilities will be endless in discovering the secrets of the universe. As your dream world becomes more vibrant and intense, reality will become more dreamlike. Don't be alarm, this is normal, embrace this transformation.

Listen to your inner voice and stay true to yourself. It will settle itself out and you will realize that in the dreams, there are important messages for you. It is in this realm that spiritual beings will communicate with you. In this you are connecting with the power of the source, the spirit and the sub conscience. Once you get it figured out and learn to listen, there will be an empowerment that will serve you well.

**Becoming Integrity Based** - This isn't a symptom as much as it is a shift in your thinking. While you may have lived your entire life going along to get along, you will find yourself taking a stand on issues that in the past you would retreat from. This shift will surprise you as you take a stand suddenly without prior thought. This is good even at the expense of your job, career or home. It is the beginning of living an Authentic Life based in Integrity. This is where you are starting to listen to your inner intuitive voice. No longer will you stand by and allow injustice to take place. You will no longer want to be associated with dishonest people or companies.

Word of caution, insure that it is your intuitive voice, your inner heart guiding you and not your Ego. If you feel that your Authentic self is compelling you to take action, then so do. How do you know the difference? Ask yourself if there is guilt involved in the decision, if operating out of spirit, there will be no guilt. There is no guilt in attaining spiritual awakening.

**Closing Comments** - While they are several more symptoms, these will give you an overview of what to expect in the event that an awakening happens to you. Remember, do not be afraid. Recognize it for what it is, surrender to the moments and ask how you may learn from them. Let go and go with the flow and enjoy the ride the best you can. While this is going on, a sense of Oneness and a synchronicity with the divine source is taking place, embrace this time.

# Chapter Six

## Indigos on Awareness and Enlightenment

*"Everything had changed suddenly-the tone, the moral climate; you didn't know what to think, whom to listen to. As if all your life you had been led by the hand like a small child and suddenly you were on your own, you had to learn to walk by yourself. There was no one around, neither family nor people whose judgment you respected. At such a time you felt the need of committing yourself to something absolute-life or truth or beauty-of being ruled by it in place of the man-made rules that had been discarded. You needed to surrender to some such ultimate purpose more fully, more unreservedly than you had ever done in the old familiar, peaceful days, in the old life that was now abolished and gone for good."*          *— Boris Pasternak, Doctor Zhivago*

Awareness and Enlightenment is not something that needs to be attained. You cannot attain that which you already have. You were born with the Divine Perfection of God. The light of the divine source is and has been always within. All that is needed is a shift in perspective to see this truth. That shift is Ascension. Ascension is rising above the illusion of this world to discover your true essence of being. By changing your perspective by rising above the trappings of the material world you will create a higher state of conscious awareness. As you become aware of this change you will realize that you are not your body or your ego. You will come to know that you are pure conscious and awareness connected to the divine source that is beyond all description, all expression and all definition. In the realization of this absolute divine love comes the awareness and enlightenment followed by a great compassion.

When you reach that level of awareness and enlightenment you are in that field beyond illusion, a state beyond the mind, you will begin to become misunderstood by others. Your own family and closest friends will no longer understand you. That is a guarantee! But not to worry, that is normal and to be expected.

Once you discover living beyond the mind, you'll be unable to convey to them your new found discovery using their language. Even though it can't be done, you will still try. You'll try to say what cannot be said. You'll try to express what cannot be expressed. You'll try to define what cannot be defined. The reasons for these acts of futility will be your great compassion for them. The moment you reach that place in that field beyond the mind where all the Great Masters reside, you'll receive the gift of great compassion. It will be as if your eyes open for the first time in your life and you see the truth, the beauty and the divine love. This state has been illustrated over the centuries by the Great Masters.

Rumi the great Sufi Poet said,

*"There is a field. Out beyond ideas of wrong doings and right doings, there is a field. I'll meet you there. When the soul lies down in the grass, the world is too full to talk about. Ideas, language, even the phrase "each other" doesn't make any sense."*

---

Are you an Indigo?

One facet of that truth is great compassion. That great compassion is feed by the witness of the unnecessary suffering of others and knowing that their suffering is of their own creation. Seeing their blindness while they stumble in the dark consumed by their own fears and nightmares will cause your compassion to overflow. You'll want to tell them that they alone are responsible for creating the misery and agony that they are experiencing. You'll want to shed light on their torment and suffering as being of their own doing. You'll become bewildered and exasperated as you try to tell them that there is a way out of this hell that they live in. You'll shout to the heavens to them that this isn't the life they have to settle for. And for the most part, it will fall on deaf ears.

Plato's Allegory of a Cave best describes the frustration of this task to those who become enlightened. I encourage all to read this story to get an understanding of this age old issue with becoming enlightened. In the story Plato states that it is possible to lead those out of the darkness and into the light. That it is philosophically possible to go from an unenlightened state to an enlightened state and to help others into that state of enlightenment. This need to help your fellow man find the truth is fueled by the great compassion of awareness and enlightenment.

You'll try to bring light to the blind. However trying to describe light to a blind person is an arduous task. You'll take on this seemingly strenuous burden out of that compassion. Making your task more difficult will be trying to describe and explain light to a blind person that has never seen light. It is like trying to describe the color, smell, taste and texture of an orange to someone that has never experienced an orange. There is just no way to convey the meaning of that orange to someone that hasn't had that experience.

Another way of putting it is to imagine that you have never been to a beach. You can read all the books on beaches, watch all the movies that have beaches in them, talked to people that have been to a beach but until you yourself are standing there on a beach, feeling the surf caressing your feet as you stand at the break, feeling the interaction of the water and sand as it dances around your feet with the smell of the saltwater in the breeze, until then, you will never really know. You must experience it yourself to grasp the real meaning of being on a beach.

It is the same for awareness and enlightenment. It is an experience that must bear witness to the individual for that individual to truly comprehend the meaning of it. What people need is not intellect and logic to understand. They need the sensation of the experience to understand. They need their eyes opened.

The difference between being aware and enlighten is you know that you are only knowing and awareness. You know that you are just part of the source and the source at the same time. There is no past or future, that the past, future and the present all reside in the now. You are reflective energy capable of seeing it all within the source.

It is quoted that Buddha said,

*"I am not a man or a god. I am not an animal, not a tree, not a rock. I am awareness, just pure awareness, just a mirror reflection of all that is."*

Within this awareness is the great compassion that arrives on the coattails of enlightenment, at that moment your eyes are finely opened. There is only one path you can take that will enable you to open your eyes and regain your sight. That path is for you to go to that field, that state that is beyond the mind. You must move pass the constraints of intellect and logic. You need to break free of the preconditioning taught to you by the rulers of society and rise above this false ideology. You need to realize that you are not your thoughts, not your ego and not your body.

The primary issue with this ideology, this preconditioning by society is society teaches the masses from birth to be blind. Society needs blind people. Unaware blind people make good slaves. They are taught to blindly follow the dogmas of religion, the dogmas of polities, and the dogmas of education. All these dogmas have been formulated to manipulate the people. The masses are dependent on their leaders for their thoughts and their life's. They are taught to believe that whatever falls outside the narrow boundaries of these imposed beliefs is to be dismissed as nonsense. In this manner the people will remain obedient and submissive to the whims of their leaders, whether those leaders are their priest, politicians or educators.

Some people in this system may get a misguided clue as to the reality and wish to become a leader. The framework of the system allows for the blind to elect other blind people to positions of power, a blind inferior system that is governed by other blind inferior people. Whether it is politicians, educators or men of religion, for the most part, it is the blind leading the blind.

In this system people are completely unaware of themselves. They know everything else; strive to learn all there is to know to the best of their knowledge except for one critical aspect, their own selves.

In the words of Carl Jung,

*"People will do anything no matter how absurd to stop from facing their souls."*

People will fool themselves into believing that they know themselves and therein lays their biggest mistake. They see their bodies, hear their speech, think with their minds, experience their character and witness their behavior. With all of this said, this still isn't who they truly are. They are unconscious of their conscious, unaware of any awareness so therefore they live life in a state of illusion. With these belief systems, illusions come easily.

At the heart of this system is education. It is through the education system that these false beliefs are engrained. One way the conspiracy is perpetrated is with language. The ability to communicate is near impossible. Parents cannot communicate with their children, a husband cannot communicate with his wife, and co-workers cannot communicate with each other in the workplace. Words take on their own meanings even within the same household. Communication is difficult. It is a corruption of language at play.

Language is the means in which we communicate and exchange our thoughts. The way in which we use language at its most fundamental core affects how we view the world. We live in a world constructed by language. Language reflects thought; well at least that it is the purpose of language. The way we see and describe the world is directly related to how we use language. The reality is language has been corrupted since its inception.

Socrates the great philosopher never wrote anything down. Socrates believed the written word was too vulnerable to misinterpretation. His thoughts were anyone reading it may have a different perspective as to the meaning of the words. There for creating a completely different interpretation of the story. Language represents our experiences, the breakdown comes from everyone's experiences are different. For example take the word "dog". This word would have a completely different meaning for a boy living in the Mid-West, to an Eskimo, for a hunter in England or a Swiss Mountain Rescuer. How this applies to the aware and enlighten towards those who are in the dark can be best said by William Bramley,

*"The transformation of spiritual knowledge into a system of obscure symbols had a devastating impact on human society. This misidentification is so strong today that almost all studies of spirit or spiritual phenomena are lumped into such disgraced classifications as Occultism, Spiritualism or*

*Witchcraft. The attempt thousands of years to keep spiritual knowledge out of the hands of the profane has almost entirely destroyed the credibility and unity of that knowledge."*

The destructive potential of language is contained within the very nature of interpretation and representation. A word, particularly a noun of a unique object is processed into a finite number of categories. By lumping together unique words in this manner, the words lose their essence and meaning that made them unique in the first place. These reformed words deny the uniqueness of each moment and each experience, reducing it to a "this" or a "that" They grant us the power to manipulate and control with logic the things they refer to. Language also reasserts the presence of the ego through the use of pronouns creating a speaker and listener dialect. The real issue being that every experience is being interpreted differently by the observers and there for creating the confusion in the interpretation and representation.

Language as you can see is only one of the conflicts of the Enlighten in trying to communicate with the unenlightened. As you try to speak to the blind using their language, the problem is by the time their mind grabs hold of the words, the meaning has changed. You are trying to communicate something that you found in that field beyond the mind where all thoughts disappear, where you yourself disappear, where egos cease to exist.

In the field there is absolute silence, absolute peace, and absolute connective-ness to the divine source. Now, how do you bring this infinite experience into words? You don't. There are no words to describe this indescribable. This is why you will be misunderstood, that is guaranteed.

Being aware and enlightened you must become a compassionate teacher. There are three steps you can use to help those along the path to self discovery. These steps will help in showing them the way. Remember that all of us were born with the built in abilities to be awaken and become aware. We all were born with eyes that we can open at anytime. This path that you take in great compassion for others will be followed by patience, tolerance, and understanding.

The first step is to learn how to meditate. Teach the value of meditation. Mediation is the art of opening ones' eyes. Through meditation spiritual knowledge is learned by feeling, by experiencing not by logic. It is in the un-cluttering of the mind that room is made for the Divine to come in. Through meditation, the years of the preconditioning can start to be stripped away. In releasing from the preconditioning and becoming an individual one can start on the path to becoming enlightened.

The next stop on the path to awareness and enlightenment is to become a disciple, a follower of the truth, a student learning to reconnect to the divine source. Every individual will find their own truth in their own way. In order to start on this quest, one must set aside all of their prejudices and finely break free from the constraints of the group think of society. They must learn to listen to what is said in the silence of meditation without any words being spoken. They must train their mind not to listen to their mind or their mind's interpretations. Rather learn to feel the experience of divine love like one would listen to the breeze passing through the trees or listening to the sound of running water in a brook or listening to classical music. This is the state that they must train their mind to be in order to advance on the path, freeing the mind from the mind.

As one begins to obtain awakening and awareness through mastering these steps in being a disciple, a follower of the truth, their next step on the path is becoming a devotee. A devotee is one who has not only learned to drop the mind but has also learned to bring their heart into the process. A sign of mastering the fundamentals of being a disciple is learning to listen to the heart from a perspective of love instead of a position of logic. Becoming a devotee is within itself a fulfillment of being a disciple. Only a few people will master this level of being a devotee. Those who do will begin to understand the being of awareness and enlightenment. At this point a great compassion will overtake the individual and a transformation will take place. In this world of just being, of liberation, light and love, they will understand through feeling, that this language has no words. They will hear the sounds in the silence, the nirvana in the unspoken language of the Divine Loving Source.

This is your task, your purpose in life. Having become aware and enlightened, to use your great compassion along with your knowledge to help those who desire to strive to become enlightened themselves. Along the journey you will learn the meaning of joyful surrender, loving kindness, unconditional love, being nonjudgmental. The benefits are the mastering the art of patience, tolerance, and understanding. In the course of your service, your reward will be in becoming a Buddha in your own right; you'll become just pure awareness connected with the Divine Source.

*"Lara walked along the tracks following the path worn by pilgrims and then turned in the fields. Here she stopped and, closing her eyes, took a deep breath of the flower-scented air of the broad expanse around her. It was dearer to her than her kin, better than a lover, wiser than a book. For a moment she rediscovered the purpose of her life. She was here on earth to grasp the meaning of enchantment and to call each thing by its right name, or, if this were not within her power, to give birth out of love for life to successors that would do it in her place."* — *Doctor Zhivago*

# Chapter Seven

## Science and the Indigo

### The Metaphysics of Quantum Physics for Indigos

*"If you're scientifically literate, the world looks very different to you. And that understanding empowers you"*
— *Neil deGrasse Tyson, Astrophysicist*

**The Indigo and the Collective Universe** - Indigos are individual souls. You will retain your identity. That is part of the dualistic nature that we all live in. As you grow in awareness, you will be able to participate with the collective universe of which you are a part. As you improve your gifts and powers, so too you will improve the collective. While the collective universe is far more infinite than anyone can imagine, the collective is aware of all its parts and all the parts are aware of the collective. As you grow, so does the collective. It is in this constant creating and growing, that you bring forth the awareness of the collective as a whole and grow.

You can consider the Collective Universe as being interconnected to any and all life forms. You need to be aware of this interconnectedness. Every action, every word, every thought has an effect on the collective. I like the way Thich Nhat Hanh, the famous Vietnamese Zen Master put it,

*"We carry in our heart not only our personal joys and sorrows, but also the joys and sorrows that are society itself. When you take action that brings well-being for yourself, you bring about well-being for the world."*

Let's take a look at the Collective Universe from the viewpoint of Quantum Physics. If you grasp this concept from the perspective of Physics, it might clear the way for you to become more intertwine within the Collective Universe. By showing you how all of this works in relationship to you, you will begin to understand how to manifest and create from the Collective Universe. I want to start off with a quote from Albert Einstein.

*"Reality is an illusion, albeit a persistent one."*
— *Albert Einstein*

**Quantum Entanglement / We are all connected** - In Quantum Physics one can see that the sub atomic world is so much more stranger than the world we live in. In Quantum Entanglement, the quantum states of two or more objects have a reference to each other, regardless of the distance between them. They act as one even though they are separated. The objects are always connected and act as one. This goes back to the Buddhist belief of the Indra' net. The belief is that everything in the universe is interconnected, whatever happens to one part of the net, happens to the entire net. Francis Harold Cook describes the metaphor of the Indra's net as follows, "Far away in the heavenly abode of the great god Indra, there is a wonderful net which has been hung by some cunning artificer in such a manner that it stretches out infinitely in all directions. In accordance with the extravagant taste of deities, the artificer has hung a single glittering jewel in each "eye" of the net, and since the net itself is infinite in dimension, the jewels are infinite in number. There hang the jewels, glittering like stars in the first magnitude, a wonderful sight to behold. If we now arbitrarily select one of these jewels for inspection and look closely at it, we will discover that in its polished surface there are reflected all the other jewels in the net, infinite in number. Not only that, but each of the jewels reflected in this one jewel is also reflecting all other jewels, so that there is an infinite reflecting process occurring."

It is incredible that within ancient religious text you can find such a poetic description of a modern day theory of Quantum Entanglement. The Hindus and the Buddhist both believed eons ago in the interconnectedness of the universe. Now with today's science we are coming full circle. This is why this is important to Indigos. Indigos have a sense of connection and understanding with all living creatures and nature. Maybe they don't know the why, but the feeling is still there. These feelings of connection are based in science and in history. There is no separation other than the separation in our minds that we created out of ignorance.

**The Copenhagen Interpretation / You create your own Universe** - Now let's take a look at the Copenhagen Interpretation. The Copenhagen Interpretation was proposed by Niels Bohr in 1920. His theory was a quantum particle doesn't exist in one state or another but exist in all possible states at once. It is only when we go to observe the particle that the particle is forced to choose one probability. Since we might choose to view the particle in different ways, the particle is forced to behave erratically conforming to the state in which we are viewing the particle, when we are not viewing the object, it is existing in all possible states at the same time; this is called "coherent superposition". All possible states of the object that can exist, exist in a particle form or in a wave function. When we observe the object, the superposition collapses and the object is forced into a state that we can see.

This brings us to "Schrondinger's Cat" The famous thought experiment introduced in 1935 by physicist Erwin Schrodinger. In his experiment, Schrodinger puts his cat into a box with a piece of radioactive material and a Geiger counter to detect any radiation. When the Geiger counter detects the decay of the radioactive material, it would release a hammer that would break a flask containing hydrocyanic acid. Upon release of the acid, the vapors would kill the cat. Once the cat is sealed into the box, the cat begins to exist in an unknowing state. Since we cannot observe the cat in the sealed box, we cannot say with any certainty if the cat is alive or dead. So, according to the theory, the cat is both alive and dead at the same time. Reminds me of the saying, if a tree falls in the forest and no one is around to hear it, does it make a sound? The summary here is, until the object is observed it can exist in any form.

What does this have to do with you? Simple, the quantum states remain in a state of uncertainty until there is an observer. Another way of putting this is, without consciousness to decide what to observe, there cannot be a wave function collapse which translates into no reality. The outcome is only determined at the time of the wave function collapse when you decide to view it. This means that you, you control how the universe is formed. You are the creator of your universe. Where ever you place your focus and attention, whatever you decide to think about, whether it is what you want or what you don't want, you are creating. This is why it is so important to be mindful of your thoughts. You are creating your world, unknowingly or knowingly. Decide to be aware and know that you control this power!

**Cymatics** - In studying Cymatics which is the study of visible sound and vibration or wave phenomena you will soon discover the beautiful symmetry of nature at play. In Cymatics, experiments are conducted using audible sounds to excite a medium such as powders like corn starch, salt and sugar to using liquids and mixtures of both. When the medium is excited, images begin to appear creating forms and patterns. The higher the frequency, the more complex the patterns become. Interestingly, several patterns will be the same found throughout nature, art and architecture. At higher rates of vibration, the more complex the patterns becomes within the medium. So, the higher the rate of vibration and energy, the higher state of being. It would stand to reason that if we can witness this effect on the natural world with audible sounds, imagine the power of this effect on you at levels of vibration that are beyond our auditory senses.

The world you see around you is vibrating at the same frequency as you. Everything is moving in cycles in vibrating patterns that are integral to the universe. Your senses can only perceive what you have been attuned to. Everything with mass including yourself creates an electromagnetic field of repulsion. Your body generates this repulsion effect from the energy around you to create the illusion of solid matter. Matter is not solid; it is mostly empty space just like you. Your brain translates the energy frequency and turns the electrical impulses and frequencies into a perceivable solid material world. Everything is vibrating on a frequency and pattern.

*"We have all been wrong. What we have called matter is energy, whose vibration has been so lowered as to be perceptible to the senses."* — *Albert Einstein*

*"If you want to find the secrets of the Universe, think in terms of Energy, Frequency, and Vibration."*
— *Nicolas Tesla*

Plato said that our world is shadow like and is a representation of a deeper realm of archetypes and ideals. Most of what actually exist you can't see with your eyes. Your eyes are only able to perceive a very small part of visual light frequencies. Luminous light is the only light that we can see without aid. Therefore, we must accept that there is more out there than the eye can see. Just because the eye can't see it doesn't mean it isn't there. With the aid of equipment we can see the difference of visible and invisible light by determining the wavelength { type of light } and the amplitude { intensity of the light } What this tells us is there is a multitude of frequencies and vibration in the universe. The higher the frequency, the higher the energy. This is important to understanding how energy works.

Consider for a moment that you are a radio. If you are an AM radio, all you will be able to pick up will be AM stations. Now if you are an AM/FM radio not only will you get the AM stations but the FM stations as well. What we want to become is not just an AM/FM radio but a radio that can detect all frequencies like a shortwave ham radio. We have the equipment built into ourselves. All we need to do is activate it. And that comes from developing the awakening and awareness that we have the power to do so. The vibration and frequency of manifestation is operating at the highest frequencies. Through study, self reflection, meditation and practice you can begin to turn up your own radio dial.

Another point to consider here is this. There is an electromagnetic field around every living being. In the electromagnetic field of every human being is a standing wave of vortex energy.

The vortex is part of sacred geometry. It is within this field of vortex energy that we all live. It is this force that creates our being. Every energy frequency in this dimension is operating within the vortex including thought. It is here where thought dwells and the self becomes self aware. Thought creates a set of pre sets for the vortex to work off. Matter follows these pre set flows of the energy. When we gain mastery over our true self, the singularity of who we are, then we can control the pre sets. The singularity lives in the center of the vortex. This is where the soul resides. This is where we come from and where we will return to. It is at this spot that with the mastery we can create the world we desire to live in. It is mastery over matter through thought. Many who have walked on this planet have mastered this including Jesus, Yoganada, Theresa Neumann, St Pantaleon, and many more.

Gregg Braden, in his book, Divine Matrix, recounts a story where a woman in a clinic in Beijing had an inoperable life threatening tumor. Gregg got to witness the miraculous healing of the tumor without any medicine. The only action was the chanting of a healing prayer of these intensely focused people. The key to the healing is the ability to focus emotion and energy in our bodies or that of a loved one in a noninvasive and compassionate way. This is a demonstration of the power of thought in action. When you can raise your own state of vibration, you in turn raise the state of vibration of those around you. These folks in China have mastered this art of creating healing through raising the state of being with divine vibration.

While according to Gregg, what he saw would be considered a miracle by Western Medicine, it is something that makes perfect sense within the holographic context of the Divine Matrix. I encourage everyone to read Gregg Braden's book, The Divine Matrix, for a more in depth look at this subject.

**Sacred Geometry** - In Sacred Geometry there are several numbers that are considered sacred. Pi is 3.14. The Golden Ratio is 1.68. The Fibonacci numbers, 0, 1,1 ,2, 3, 5, 8, 13, 21, 34, 55, 89, 144. The ratio of the Fibonacci numbers is 1.68, the golden ratio. If you take two of the numbers in sequence and form a Golden Rectangle. Within a Golden rectangle you can form squares and rectangles into infinity. With those squares and rectangles you can form the Golden Spiral. Now what is interesting about the Golden Spiral is it is in all of nature, from the Milky Way Galaxy to the nautilus shell to the sunflower. Indigos seem to have a connection to Sacred Geometry even when they don't understand the why. It is believed by many to be the language of God. Now for those of you that understand Sacred Geometry will get this point. In Sacred Geometry, it is the circle that is considered to be the most pure shape in the universe. With no end or beginning, unchanging, always has been and will always be. The circle in its oneness is God-Like in this manner. The circle has a timeless reality to it. Now, let's take two circles formed on a common radius. In the overlap of the two circles lays the Vesica Piscis. It is within the Vesica Piscis that everything that exists in the universe is born out of. It is called the womb of the universe. The Vesica Piscis is the creation of duality from a singular world. Let that sink in for a moment. The paradox of the Vesica Piscis is it belongs to both circles while maintaining its own identity. Not only can the Vesica Piscis relate to both worlds and itself, it also contains worlds within itself. This is the key! You are the Vesica Piscis. You belong to both worlds and contain within yourself another world. But all worlds are connected. Now think about the words of Jesus from John 14:20 in the American King James version.

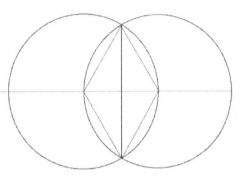

*"At that day you shall know that I am in my Father and you in me, and I in you."*

Another statement from the American King James Version that applies to making the point of singularity. This verse is from Luke 17:21

*"Neither shall they say, See here! or, see there! For, behold, the kingdom of God is within you."*

Now, what this means is, one, you are a spiritual being having a human experience, I am in my Father, and you in me, and I in you. This also means that the Vesica Piscis is in the Trilogy of which you are a part of. Second, the kingdom of God is within you. This is the world that is within the Vesica Piscis that is within you.

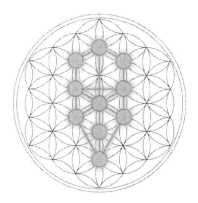

Let's take a look at the Kabbalah Tree of Life. The design is derive from concentric circles based on circles of common radius. Within the Tree of Life you'll see the Vesica Piscis. Notice the infinity of the design, you can move out from the image and retain the design as well as preserving the design by closing in on the design. The design contains 10 circles, called Sephirot connected by 22 paths. The concept of the Tree is to represent existence and creation and how universal energy transformed into the world. The Tree is about the manifested universe. The subject of the Tree if Life is deep and while it deserves more time, the point I am making here is Sacred Geometry has been recognized by Mystics since the dawn of time. The number of paths, 22, is a sacred number within the book of Zohar, the cornerstone book of Kabbalah. The Zohar states that God made the world using the Hebrew alphabet. The letters represent symbols in the creation of the world. There are 22 letters and 7 basic shapes to the letters. 22 over 7 gives you Pi 3.14. Pi is a Sacred Number.

No matter what you choose to believe or anyone else for that fact, you cannot escape from who and what you are. You are bound by the laws of the universe. These God laws dictate that you are interconnected with the source. This is why so many Indigos become attracted to Sacred Geometry. It is in Sacred Geometry that contains the sacred language of God. Indigos might not understand the reason why, but there is a deep knowing within the soul that wants that awakening and reconnection back to source.

We already have one foot in each world. We only need to wake up and realize it. Once we realize this simple law, we will be able to harness the power that is our right. We are all a true essence in spirit, but we have been fooled into believing the Ego. We are already immortal, that is a universal truth. It is the illusion of this world and the Ego that tells us otherwise.

We are pure energy, like god is pure energy. We are nothing more than that. From where we originated from, we will return. God has always been, will always be, cannot be destroyed, multiplied or created, just like energy, it goes on forever. Once this truth becomes a reality to you, then you will lose all fear of death and separation from God. How can you be separated from the source when you contain the source?

Yes, the Ego is the roadblock in preventing this truth from becoming evident. Overcome the illusion and defeat the Ego and know that you are truly a child of God, a brother or sister to Jesus. And like your brother, you too can perform any and all miracles with nothing more than this knowledge and faith that you hold this power.

**Understanding the connection to Sacred Geometry** - I want to share with you another view of what we have discussed about the Esoteric Art of Living and Sacred Geometry. One of the most common questions I receive from Indigos is the desire to understand the connection with certain shapes in nature and the meaning of them. This is a wonderful question because it shows that there is an awakening to the divine universe. Having this affinity shows a longing to connect to nature, to get back to the divine grace of the perfection of the source.

I am going to offer you the perspective of the Native American Indians. Within their beliefs, philosophy, and understanding lies a profound wisdom that every Indigo can relate to and benefit from. The Native Americans understood the power of Sacred Geometry. Their life was based on the most common principles of the universe. While they lived a simple life, their understanding of the laws of the universe was profound. We can learn a lot about how to view and live life in their teachings. Without a doubt, the Native American Indians had a crystal clear Indigo way of the seeing the world.

Black Elk of the Sioux Nation was born in 1863. He was considered to possessed unique spiritual power. This power was recognized by everyone that met him. He had been instructed in his youth in the sacred traditions of his people by the Shamans of his tribe. His father was a medicine man as well as several of his brothers. These quotes are from his autobiography, "Black Elk Speaks, Being the life story of a Holy Man of the Oglala Sioux" as told through John G. Neihardt. They pertain to the configuration of the circle and the fundamental place that the circle held in the life's of the Indian.

*"You have noticed that everything an Indian does is in a circle, and that is because the Power of the World always works in circles, and everything tries to be round. In the old days when we were a strong and happy people, all our power came to us from the sacred hoop of the nation and so long as the hoop was unbroken the people flourished. The flowering tree was the living center of the hoop, and the circle of the four quarters nourished it. The east gave peace and light, the south gave warmth, the west gave rain, and the north with its cold and mighty wind gave strength and endurance. This knowledge came to us from the other world with our religion. Everything the Power of the World does is done in a circle. The sky is round and I have heard that the earth is round like a ball and so are the stars. The wind, in its greatest power, whirls. Birds make their nest in circles, for theirs is the same religion as ours. The sun comes forth and goes down again in a circle. The moon does the same, and both are round."*

*"Even the seasons form a great circle in their changing, and always come back again to where they were. The life of a man is a circle from childhood to childhood and so it is in everything where power moves. Our tepees were round like the nest where the Great Spirit meant for us to hatch our children. And while I stood there I saw more than I can tell and I understood more than I saw; for I was seeing in a sacred manner the shapes of all things in the spirit, and the shape of all shapes as they must live together like one being. And I say the sacred hoop of my people was one of the many hoops that made one circle, wide as daylight and as starlight, and in the center grew one mighty flowering tree to shelter all the children of one mother and one father."*

As you can see Black Elk had a deep understanding of the world. In his words you can see the relationship of Sacred Geometry in his world. This is what the Indigo is searching for, that deep understanding of the real and true world.

Below is a quote from Ohiyesa, also known as Charles Eastman. He is best known for his work in helping form the Boy Scouts of America. Ohiyesa grew up on a reservation in Minnesota, later becoming a doctor, graduating from Boston University in 1889. He went on to do great things for the Indian. I would recommend reading his biography. Here he talks about the differences between the Whites and the Indians. Notice the deep conviction and understanding of the importance to being connected to nature.

*"As a child I understood how to give; I have forgotten this grace since I became civilized. I lived the natural life, whereas I now live the artificial. Any pretty pebble was valuable to me then; every growing tree an object of reverence. Now I worship with the white man before a painted landscape whose value is estimated in dollars! Thus the Indian is reconstructed, as the natural rocks are ground to powder and made into artificial blocks which may be built into the walls of modern society."*

*"The first {Native} American mingled with his pride a singular humility. Spiritual arrogance was foreign to his nature and teaching. He never claimed that the power of articulate speech was proof of superiority over the dumb creation; on the other hand, it is to him a perilous gift. He believes profoundly in silence- the sign of a perfect equilibrium. Silence is the absolute poise or balance of body, mind and spirit. The man who preserves his selfhood is ever calm and unshaken by the storms of existence- not a leaf, as it were, astir on the tree; not a ripple upon the surface of the shining pool- his, in the mind of the unlettered sage, is the ideal attitude and conduct of life."*

## Solfeggio Frequencies and the Indigo -

*"God built the universe with Numbers."* — Pythagoras

**Solfeggio Frequencies and the Indigo** - This is important for Indigos to understand. Solfeggio Frequencies ties into Sacred Geometry and Cymatics. 70% of the human body is comprised of water. Water reacts to vibration and frequency. Doctor Masaru Emoto has done extensive research into this field. His book, "Messages from Water "shows how water exposed to thoughts take on an appearance based on the energy level of the thoughts. Water exposed to loving thoughts once frozen would have a beautiful crystalline structure where water exposed to lower level thoughts would appear to have an ugly structure. The higher the state of emotion the more complex the design would be. Lower states created designs that were not complex or orderly. The point to this is everything in life is interconnected. It is very important to be aware of the affects of emotions and feelings on the human body. It has been shown that what affects us mentally also affects us physically. This is where the Solfeggio Frequencies come in. Look at the diagram of the Solfeggio Frequencies. Notice that the numbers transpose to create the other numbers, 174, 417, and 741. This is considered to be a part of the intelligent design of creation.

As you become aware of Sacred Geometry and aspects of the subject, you will see how all of this is interconnected and how it plays into being an Indigo. There is a reason for this divine science. Now for a little background history as to what Solfeggio Frequencies are. I have included this article from David Hulse, who has done tremendous research into the field of Solfeggio Frequencies. Once you read this information, you'll see the connection.

## History of Solfeggio Frequencies by David Hulse, SomaEnergetics.com

These original sound frequencies were apparently used in Ancient Gregorian Chants, such as the great hymn to St. John the Baptist, along with others that church authorities say were lost centuries ago. The chants and their special tones were believed to impart tremendous spiritual blessings when sung in harmony during religious masses. These powerful frequencies were rediscovered by Dr. Joseph Puleo as described in the book Healing Codes for the Biological Apocalypse by Dr. Leonard Horowitz. I give honor to both of these gentlemen for the part they've played in helping return these lost frequencies back to humanity.

**The Six Solfeggio Frequencies include:**

UT – 396 Hz – Liberating Guilt and Fear
RE – 417 Hz – Undoing Situations and Facilitating
Change
MI – 528 Hz – Transformation and Miracles (DNA Repair)
FA – 639 Hz – Connecting/Relationships
SOL – 741 Hz – Awakening Intuition
LA – 852 Hz – Returning to Spiritual Order

For example, the third note, frequency 528, relates to the
note MI on the scale and derives from the phrase "MI-ra
gestorum" in Latin meaning "miracle." Stunningly, this is
the exact frequency used by genetic biochemists to repair
broken DNA – the genetic blueprint upon which life is
based!

**A Little History -**

At the turn of the century the awareness of DNA entered
the collective consciousness of the world. We have incarnat-
ed into this human experience as divine beings with a blueprint, a set of instructions. We know that a very small percentage (3%) of those instructions make up our physiology.

Carl Sagan writes that most of our genetic information
*(about 97%)* is unused DNA. He refers to this as "genetic
gibberish." Is it possible that most of who we are still lies
dormant as our human potential?

In the old paradigm of religion, "potential" remained a mystery to the human mind, therefore we coined a mystical
term called "SPIRIT." "Spirit" was something that was
detached from who we were, something we didn't have and
could only be gained through the systems of most religions.
The old paradigm and its premise stated that we began as
biology in the womb of our mothers. Telliard deChardin
tells us that we are not a human being trying to attain a
spiritual experience, but, rather, we are spiritual beings

having a human experience. This shift in perception causes a tremendous difference in the way we perceive ourselves in this third/fourth time-space continuum.

Being a student of "A Course In Miracles" in the late 80's, I was faced with a dichotomy in the idea that we are not a body. I never understood this statement fully until I read a quotation by Albert Einstein which stated:"Concerning matter, we have been all wrong. What we have called matter is energy, whose vibration has been so lowered as to be perceptible to the senses. There is no matter." I believe what is being stated is that at the deepest level we are not separate, as a body, as a spirit, as a soul — we are just energy-beings. This is the level of consciousness being opened to us from which a new paradigm is emerging for the purpose of healing all separation. The popular term, "The Divine is in me"- makes "me" separate from the Divine. May I suggest a shift in the saying to: "The Divine, AS me" to remove the separation.

As we move from genetics and concepts like Soul, "Soul Mates" and "Soul work," we move beyond physical diagnosis, into a new field of quantum physics. In this new field, where consciousness is seen as a unified field where everything is everything else, *(T.O.E. Theory – The Theory of Everything)* —there are no boundaries. There is no "this" or "that;" no you or me. It is a pure field of awareness – consciousness. I solved the dichotomy about "we are not our body" by changing my perception of genetics to energetics – realizing that we are not meant to ignore our physiology, but recognize the body as energy, vibrating at a very dense frequency.

## How Did The Solfeggio Frequencies Get Lost?

I discovered that these powerful frequencies had been given to the church many years ago for a very spiritual purpose. This was back when the church was a wonderful place for the people in the villages to gather together. The church served as a social, political, and spiritual place. People came to Mass, which at that time, was done in Latin *(until Vatican II came along)*.

When people sing in Latin or musical tones, it is very powerful, because it gets through all of the limited thought forms, and into deeper levels of the subconscious – accessing insights beyond belief systems.

As described above by Dr. Candice Pert, PhD, energy and vibration go all the way to the molecular level. She states that we have 70 different receptors on the molecules and when vibration and frequency reaches that far they begin to vibrate. Moreover, she observed, "as they begin to vibrate they sort of touch each other, and tickle each other, and they play and mount each other." It's this whole energetic dance ritual, at the cellular level, that opens the chromosomes and exposes the DNA to the frequencies. When we do toning, drumming, chanting, or tuning forks – it can be a way to direct energy for transformational purposes.

Vibration and sound can be used, like most things, either with positive intention or negative intention. Used negatively, it's nothing more than control and manipulation. Most of the world has been built upon control and manipulation by the way we communicate thru language. A lot of different texts, such as the Bible, talk about the importance of just making Sound—whether it's chants, drumming, or speaking in tongues *(such as the charismatic fundamentalists do),* they are just different ways that people are accessing deeper levels of themselves.

**The Esoteric Art of Living** - By now you should realize that you are a Spiritual Being having a Human Experience. It is difficult to manage living in two worlds at once. While as much as we want to stay in the spiritual world, we are here and forced to deal with the issues of life. With that said we can still make our time here a little more comfortable once we understand the secret of the esoteric art of living. The secret is simple. It is this; you are a singularity living in a dualistic world. Wow, let's look at that again, for something simple, it doesn't make much sense. We are all a singularity living in a dualistic world. This means we have one foot in each world.

What is required to make this work is creating balance in your life. One of the keys in doing this is somewhat of a paradox. You should not take yourself so seriously but do take what you do seriously. In not taking yourself so seriously in life you will develop the art of letting go. You will realize that problems are coming and going and will learn to deal with them for what they are, just another aspect of life.

We discussed dealing with problems earlier in the book but warrants mention again. Remember to practice common sense and come from a mindset of finding solutions instead of being in a state of blame. The way to learn to deal with problems is to ask a simple question, is this 5 minute problem, a 5 hour problem, a 5 day problem or a 5 week problem? You will also learn to ask yourself if this problem is going to matter a month from now. You'll soon discover what you have thought to be important will cease to be. Just remembering the past events of when you thought your world was coming to an end and realizing today that the worry and fret that you put into it was for nothing. Live life as if this has already happened and you know the outcome. In the end none of the problems matter other than doing your best in life in being compassionate and loving. You know that you are here to play a role.The character you're playing will change in the next play. All of what you are experiencing is the illusion and a dream. You know the reality of who you are and where you're from. By having one foot in each world you understand the meaning of, "You're in this World, not of this World"

Another point about the esoteric art is realizing that it is okay to experience negative emotions as long as you know that they cannot get to you. Become like the Buddhist believe, feel it, learn from it, get to know it and then, let it go. Just let it go. It is easy to master this when you stop taking yourself so seriously. Remember you are just playing a role in a play. Play your part, if a situation comes along that requires a negative reaction, remember it is not you that is experiencing the emotion, it is your character.

I worked with a world renowned designer who had mastered the esoteric art of living. He was a superstar in his field. He had worked with Presidents and World Leaders. He was a very distinguish well educated man originally from Europe and he had an air of refinement about him. I worked closely with him on a project and was able to spend a lot of time with him. What impress me about him was his lack of Ego and his ability to treat everyone with the same kindness and respect. I must have asked him a million questions about everything under the sun. I soon discovered that Andre had a sense of living life that I hadn't seen in anyone before. On one occasion I ask him if it was it was difficult designing for the rich and famous. He said the designing part was easy, it was dealing with the rich and famous that was the challenge. He said that he had to deal with people who had forgotten who they really were. He went on to say that these people believe that they were what the public believe them to be. They thought they were their image, they believed they were special. In other words, these people became the character in the movie and lost all connection to their true being, the Actor. They truly believe that they really were the legends that the press and public had made them into. He understood this and knew at times; he too, would have to slip into "role" in order to deal with these personalities.

He told me there were times when he needed to remind these stars that he deserve equal billing on the Marque sign too. That he was a star in his own right and when required, got that equal billing. The difference here is Andre knew it was just a role. By knowing that he was able to keep one foot in each world and not let the situation affect him.

I was blessed one day to see him in action. This gave me the understanding of what he meant. This became the foundation of the concept of the Esoteric Art of Living. On this particular day we had a meeting at the job site with the client and his entourage. Andre was having difficulties with this client. The client felt that he knew more than Andre and refused to take the advice given by Andre. At one point during the project Andre asked why he was there since his suggestions were rejected. But this day was the day that Andre slipped into "role". When the client finished with his stern thoughts Andre came undone. A fit ensued following by chairs being thrown and tables overturn along with the loud and foul language. While this commotion was being played out I was on the opposite side of the room facing the entourage. I could see the reaction on these folks as Andre told them in no uncertain terms of how he felt about the situation. Their lifeless expressions spoke volumes. About this time as Andre was turning around to face me, he gives me a wink and a smile, no one else could see this but me. It was at this moment that it became clear to me everything he had told me. I knew in an instance that he was merely playing the role he needed to play in order to insure that these "actors" knew his name belonged on the marquee in the same size letters as theirs.

After the episode played out and Andre knowing that his point had gotten across, life began to get back to normal. The clients realized that they needed to change their views on the project and let the man they hired to do his job and stay out of his way. They left and Andre came up to me with this huge smile. His first words were, "Gosh that felt great!" He gave me a pat on the back and started to help me put the pieces back together. While helping he told he that sometimes we all need to shake things up, to get the blood flowing and get people back in line with the program. To remind them that there is this thing called reality and there is a world outside their minds. He said it was a wakeup call for them I got the point of what he was saying. While he was justified getting angry and losing his cool, and while maybe he shouldn't have thrown the fit, the point is, he did not let it get to him, the real him, the actor behind the character in this scene in this particular movie. There was at all times a knowing that he was playing the part. He got to feel the anger, experience it, hold it and let it go. There were no regrets or lingering of the negative emotions. I learned a life lesson that day. One, don't hang on to negative emotions and let them festered. Two, don't take yourself too seriously. And to know how to keep true to yourself while having to play your part in this movie called life. After all it is all a dream anyway.

Like the nursery rhyme goes,

*"Row, row, row your boat. Gently down the stream. Merrily, merrily, merrily, merrily, Life is but a dream."*

That is the Esoteric Secret to the Art of Living. Everything you needed to know you already learned years ago.

**The Indigo-ness of Native Americans** - I want to touch on a few areas on the Native Americans. I have found several instances of an Indigo-ness way of thinking. I have already shown you the insights of Black Elk and George Eastman in covering other aspects of Indigos. I want to show you a few more insights to bring to your attention of how advanced these people were. It is sad how they were treated and considered a lower form of being in the eyes of the Europeans that came to this country. In reality, the Europeans that settled this land in fact were the savages. I want you to see that these Indians indeed were spiritually advanced and we all can learn a lesson from their beliefs and philosophies. We talked about quantum physics and how it all relates to ancient religious text and how it affects Indigos. Now let's look at a few examples.

The Hopi Indians in their history and prophesies they never refer to time in the linear sense that we do in their grammar. What they do is use tenses. Their past is the manifested and the future is what is going to be manifested. This includes the physical as well as the mystical. While this is a system to show a time line, it isn't in the sense that we think. Within the Hopi Nation there was no separation of the physical world or the ethereal world. It is believed that the Hopi considered thought to be an active energy capable of creating the physical world. This is an interesting perspective to contemplate considering what we have learned from modern science.

Another interesting aspect to the Native Americans is their use of language. The Navajo to mention one group have proverbs that when translated give a different meaning than one would expect. For instance, there is a Navajo proverb, "May you walk in beauty" we would take this to mean walk along the fields of flowers or through a nice pastoral setting. The truth to the saying in the Navajo language is this, walk through your day without saying anything harmful to anyone, whatever you do say; make sure it is a benefit to creating beauty in their life.

Another proverb is, "Always assume your guest is tired, cold and hungry, and act accordingly." Translated into today's language this proverb would mean for you to always come from a perspective of love and compassion. Give to another without having to be asked. To fulfill a need where there is one, to treat your fellow man with respect. Now that sounds like an attitude of merit that is for the betterment of your fellow man. This is a true Indigo characteristic.

Another side to the life of the Native Americans that reminds me of Indigo-ness is their political nature. Seems that their sense of ruling was not done with Egos coming into play nor do you see a separation of people by class. Native American tribes did not have a hierarchical form of government. The members of the tribe had jobs to do base on their skills. Whatever a particular individual was best at doing, then that is what that person did. If someone was more skilled in being a healer, then he or she becomes responsible to keeping the tribe healthy. The best skilled hunters would do the hunting and so forth. Yes, there was a leader that had the final decision in who would do what and manage the affairs of the tribe. What is important here is that within the tribe, no one would acquire more material wealth than the others. There was a sense of everyone being as important as the others. There were no Egos at play. More importantly was the collective sense that the survival, health and well-being of all individuals were as equally important to the survival to the tribe. What needs to be noted here within the tribe was that the contribution of skills from the individual was for the betterment of the tribe, not to serve a class of ruling elites or to contribute their work to a government. A true community spirit of all for one and one for all without the egotistical elites who felt they were better than others. A true sense of equality existed with respect not only for one another but for all living beings. The trappings of materialistic objects didn't hold any appeal to them. Trying to get ahead and having more than their neighbors didn't make sense to them either. But insuring that their fellow members of the tribe were well feed, secured and happy and their well-being did matter. That is another great Indigo trait.

# Chapter Eight

## Seven Steps to the Summit

**How far can you go?** Wallace Wattles said that when an organism has more life than can be expressed in the functions of its own plane, it develops the organs of a higher plane, and a new species is originated. I believe this applies to all of us too. I see no reason why anyone couldn't become whatever they desire. Literally, the sky is the limit.

While these seven steps to the Summit might be more than some Indigos wish to buy into at this moment, it is important to understand and realize how far you can go. This might not be where you are at on the path, but again, I feel that this is important enough to at least give you an outline of what can be done. Even if you don't buy into it, you have been told about the potential of what can be accomplished.

One point I would like to make is this. Read the book, "Autobiography of a Yogi, by Paramahansa Yoganada" Within the pages of this book, you will see the transformation of a normal, everyday kind of kid turn into a Spiritual Master. In my opinion, Yoganada was an Indigo who followed his heart and soul and on several occasions, went out on faith. Never was he left high and dry. All his needs were met when they needed to be. Whenever he needed to speak, the voice was always there. Anyone who believes that they are an Indigo must read this book. Yoganada will serve as a great role model.

I believe strongly that if you know who you are and where you need to go, you need a road map and Yoganada's book will serve as that road map. You will see what lies ahead and will learn through him what to expect. At times, the road will be bumpy, but it will not matter because as long as you know the end game, then nothing can stop you from getting there. It is all up to you to decide how far you want to go and how to use this information.

Another great book on this subject is by Aldous Huxley, The Perennial Philosophy. He covers how in all religions, at the core the message is the same, that we are all one, all part of the source. The only obstacle from becoming one is ourselves. This is information that has been available since the dawn of time. I recommend picking up a copy and read it. It will be an invaluable resource to you as you continue on your journey. I have included a few quotes from his book to illustrate how timeless this message is.

Everyone contains an unconscious desire to reach the summit of being and awareness. But the problem is most folks don't have the passion or motivation to pursue this goal, and that includes some Indigos. We are on the cusp of a major change and those who have become the person that they are meant to be will reap the rewards of the coming change. A change is coming, rest assured, a change to about to take place.

We were pure at birth and since then, we have gone through these environments of misinformation, mistruths, and illusions. Having lived in these lower vibrations and lower energy environments, it's no wonder we are the way we are. But we don't need to stay there any longer.

It's time to realize that we can control our environment and take charge of our lives no matter what life has thrown at us. Now is the time to get it right and get back on the path that was intended for all of us. Now is the time to purify ourselves. All that is required is a desire, a passion, an awakening to want the truth. Remember, no matter how far the journey, it all begins with a single step. With passion and focus, you will achieve the goal of getting to the summit.

I want to share the thoughts of people that have gone before us. This wisdom is as old as time itself. This is not some crazy New Age talk or some fringe ideal that someone with an over active imagination came up with. These ideals are universal and have been around for centuries.

*"The soul that is attached to anything, however much good there may be in it, will not arrive at the liberty of divine union. For whether it is a strong wire rope or a slender and delicate thread that holds the bird, it matters not, if it really holds it fast; for until the cord is broken, the bird cannot fly. So the soul, held by the bounds of human affections, however slight they may be, cannot, while they last, make its way to God."* — *St. John of the Cross c.1500*

*"When you are neither attached to, nor detached from, them, then you enjoy your perfect unobstructed freedom, then you have your seat of enlightenment."* — *Huang-Po, Zen Master c.800*

*"When is a man in mere understanding? I answer, When a man sees one thing separated from another. And when is a man above mere understanding? That I can tell you; When a man sees All in all, then a man stands beyond mere understanding."* — *Meister Eckhart c.1300*

Here is the 16th Chapter of Lao Tzu's Tao Te Ching. This illustrates the timeliness of the thoughts of man in unlocking the wisdom of the universe and attaining connection back to the source.

*Empty your minds of all thoughts.*
*Let your heart be at peace.*
*Watch the turmoil of beings,*
*but contemplate their return.*

*Each separate being in the universe*
*returns to the common source.*
*Returning to the source is serenity.*

*If you don't realize the source,*
*You stumble in confusion and sorrow.*
*When you realize where you come from,*
*you naturally become tolerant,*
*disinterested, amused,*
*kindhearted as a grandmother,*
*dignified as a king.*

*Immersed in the wonder of the Tao,*
*You can deal with whatever life brings you,*
*And when death comes, you are ready.*

**Enlightenment, Ascension and Responsibility** - Before getting into the steps I want to stress the importance of responsibility. In any faith, in order to attain enlightenment, one must become responsible. I wrote earlier about taking responsibility for your actions. It is even more important here. There is a direct correlation between the level of responsibility, enlightenment and ascension.

Let's take a look at ascension. The meaning of ascension is to rise above. When you take responsibility, you are rising above the folks that can't or will not deal with life's problems. To give you an example, let us look to Mother Teresa. She assumed the responsibility of her fellow man in the streets of Calcutta India. She did this out of love and compassion. While she worked tirelessly her entire life in service to those less fortunate, she brought awareness to the problems and issues of the sick and poor. All her success in life can be attributed to first, taking responsibility for more than herself. That in itself caused her to rise above the norm, an ascension towards being Christ-like.

Whatever you are currently putting your belief into, the situations, the conditions, the circumstances, you are creating the experiences that come out of that belief. To some degree being responsible is playing a part into it. When you are completely responsible for your life, you take complete ownership of it. In enlightenment, that ownership is unconditional, non-judgmental, all loving. When you master that ownership, when you are completely in harmony with the divine source at every level of your being, then my friend, you will have all the traits, characteristics, and power of God.

Let me give you an example of taking responsibility to that level. When Christ was on the cross, not only did he take responsibility for himself, he took responsibility for all mankind. He took that heavy burden because he could. Within that one act, Christ shows the power of responsibility. Christ, while on the cross, was in the very essence of being in the divine presence of source, God. Being at that level is what gave him the power to assume the sins of all men. This is born out of taking responsibility for more than himself. That is what being divine is, and what we all should strive for. In that state of unconditional love, we call it sacrifice while they call it giving. It is in that state of transformation, by taking responsibility, that love comes out of fear. That might be the lesson that matters most in life, learning divine love. To experience and give divine love, that very well could be the ultimate lesson.

**Step One - Searching for the Truth** - That is where you have started. It began with you picking this book up and reading it. You have had a desire to know more than you know. I hope that now, you realize that you are an Indigo and this quiz starts to make sense of your past and who you are.

You must know where you have been, where you are in order to know where you are going. Even an Indigo needs a road map to see where to go. You now know that you need to pay closer attention to your intuition. Begin to develop listening to that inner voice when it speaks. Cast aside the lies and mistruths when your inner voice exposes them.

Become more careful about what you allow into your mind. Learn to watch your thoughts and guard your mind against any thoughts that are harmful to your growth. Learn to meditate, to clear your mind of all the false teachings you have been told. Don't be afraid to ask why, seek the truth and don't buy anything at face value till you have done your homework. Seek out other Indigos to help assist in this journey. They are here to help, take advantage of the opportunities that come your way.

**Step Two – Learning and Obtaining Knowledge -** Learn to trust yourself. When your inner voice tells you this is a truth or this is where you need to be, listen. When a book or a program feels right, it's because it is. Ask questions, dig, and did deeper till you get the answers to are looking for. Remember that your truth is your truth. It might not be for everyone else and it doesn't matter, all that matters is you know the truth.

As an Indigo, you have gifts, learn to use and develop them. These gifts will be your greatest asset in the times to come. Remember, there is only so much time in a day, spend it wisely. You will notice as you grow, you will notice the changes in your questions. The questions will begin to show how you are discerning the lies you have been fed, from the truth.

Learn to prioritize your life, bring balance into it. Notice what you spend your time on. Are you spending your time on feeding your soul? Are you making the best of your time? As you bring balance into your life, you will begin to notice that your diet will improve, your health will improve, and your choices will improve as your knowledge improves. Learn all you can, the teacher will appear when the student is ready, so get ready! As you learn, you will be able to assist other Indigos coming along with you. Continue with meditating; keep on with training yourself new disciplines.

**Step Three – Creating Shifts in your Thinking** - As you arm yourself with this new found knowledge, you will need to make some minor shifts in your thinking. What you gave attention to in the past will become irreverent. You are an Indigo, a higher evolved being, start taking that into consideration. You have special gifts, and you know it, so become it. Don't doubt yourself, you have the power to do this, remember you are part of the Divine Source, you are an Indigo!

Practice living more carefully and with respect. Have respect for all living beings and things. Don't get caught up in situations that drain your energy. Learn to protect your quest, by keeping at bay, any threat that comes your way. When faced with a threat, send it love and send it along its way. Don't get caught up in idle gossip talking about others, practice inner respect towards others. Refrain from losing your focus by giving in to the flow of conversation of others that are not in harmony with your beliefs and thoughts. Practice this sense of living in a more careful and respectful manner.

Continue with the meditating and clearing your mind. By now you should start being able to listen to your heart more. You should start to notice shifts in your thinking. Learn to become more alert and mindful of your surroundings. Look for opportunities to give in a generous manner in time or money. Realizing that we are all part of the same Divine Source, you'll begin to see the perfection in all that you see around you. Within this new mind-set, you will become less judgmental towards others and more accepting of your fellow man. See the beauty in all that surrounds you; this is the reward of being more alert and mindful.

As you discover the truth about religion, you will automatically see a shift in your thinking. One aspect you will notice is that you will begin to turn inward in your faith, no longer needing the structure of organized religion. You will begin to see anger fade away and be replaced with a universal love. You will see changes in your attitude as you become more knowledgeable and aware. You will begin to understand the reason why you are here.

**Step Four – Awakening -** All the hard work that you have put into this quest will pay off in an instant. It will be spontaneous, a moment like a light turning on. At this moment of awakening, you will know that you are independent of the rules of society. The rules of indifference and skepticism that governed the masses with lose their hold on you.

Awakening means letting go of all the limiting beliefs and attitudes. The old ways cannot exist in this state of divine unconditional love. You are now your own person. You are coming into your element as an Indigo. With this awakening, you will begin to help others more. You will have this great compassion towards others. You will learn the value of practicing Loving Kindness. In taking the time to visit with the elderly and the sick, in helping in those less fortunate, in being understanding of others, you'll become a teacher, an example to others of how to live. Within these acts of Loving Kindness a sense of forgiveness and acceptance will appear.

The veil that has covered the truth will fall and you will see the illusions for what they are. You will also discover that your Ego has been your worst enemy. In mastering keeping your Ego in check, your rise to the summit will pick-up speed. The pieces that were missing will become clear and you will see how things fit into the big picture. You will begin to have those "Ah" moments more often. You will discover that your thoughts and actions are becoming more pure in nature.

One of the biggest changes in this awakening is you'll discover that all the answers that you seek will be found within. That it has always been there buried deep within your own being. It has been your Ego and your own blindness to the truth that has prevented you from this truth. Meditating will become a second nature to you now.

**Step Five – Remembering Who You truly Are -** With this awakening, you will realize that you are from and a part of the source. As an Indigo, this is what you have been waiting for. The clarity will become more prevalent. All makes sense now. The words of Jesus will be understood. "I am in you and you are in me, and I am in the Father. What I can do, you can do more." Yes, at this step, you will realize that you are becoming Christ-like.

The words, "The Kingdom is within" will now be understood. Knowledge will flow to you like never before; wisdom will be at your beckon call. Remembering that you are from the source and knowing that you will return to the source because you are part of the source will be bedrock of strength that will hold up under the worst of storms.

Joyful surrender has meaning to you as you experience true joy in this awakening. While you still might get off the path, you can see what awaits you, it is in plain view. The joy, happiness and compassion begins to radiate out from you

**Step Six – Practice Being Christ-like -** With the awakening and the remembering that you are who you are, and knowing, I am that I am, you will begin the growth towards a high level of being. Practice being more Christ-like. During this time, any remnants remaining from this material world and the clinging of the Ego will begin to fade.

Eventually, not only will you be able to communicate with all Indigos through mental telepathy, you will be able to communicate with all people. At this stage, you will be able to heal at will and begin to transform lower level humans to be higher states.

By now you have release pride and ego. You have learn to practice equanimity and working towards mastering the art of equanimity. You will be overwhelmed by the joy, love and peace in knowing how to be in the moment.

This is your purpose as an Indigo and you know it. The feelings of love are beyond any words. The constraints of this world will begin to lose its grip on you. You will have a sense of freedom from the world that can't be described.

**Step Seven – The Summit, Being -** At this level as an Indigo, you will know the Thich Nhat Hanh's, St Francis's, Yoganada's, Budda's, and the Christ of Mankind. You will be Christ-like, the ultimate goal of every human being. But you will have achieved this while still alive and in the body.

You will be able to walk in both worlds. All that has ever been, all that is and all that will be, will all be one at the same moment. No past, no present, no future, just now. At this stage, you will be able to bring humans along the path of evolution.

At this stage, you will be considered an Avatar. By just your thoughts, you will be able to manifest anything into being, by just thought, you will be able to heal from afar. You will be able to walk among the living on this plane as well as those living on the Astral plane. You are home!

**Closing notes -** Your Indigo gifts will continue to grow at an incredible rate. Along the way other gifts might pop up in an unexpected manner. You will notice that things that you have been dwelling on will begin to appear at just the right time. The synchronistic nature of life will come into a natural rhythm. Being aware of the changes and being able to adapt to them without fear or anxiety will be the key to an awarding experience. Learn to live in the moment and let your sensitive nature experience these feelings on a much deeper level.

In the word of Tony Robbins, "If life is worth living, then is it worth recording" so get a journal and record your journey. And take time to mediate and time for self reflection. No matter where you are, remember, "This too will pass" so enjoy the journey and live the life you are meant to live. Go in peace, love and joy and the world will be yours.

**The Quiz** - Before you take the quiz, keep in mind a few things. First, please be honest with yourself. To get the most out this quiz, take your time and think about your answers. Give the questions the attention they deserve. Answer the questions from your heart. This is between you and yourself and nobody else. Second, there is no right or wrong. There is only the truth. Whether you agree or disagree, there is no right or wrong, it just is what it is.

1-You seem to be more of a giver than a taker?

2-Do you have a hard time accepting help from others?

3-Do you ever "dumb down "to fit in?

4-Do you keep your thoughts to yourself when among others because you know they wouldn't understand?

5-Denied your true self in order to get along?

6-You have feelings that you don't belong?

7-Knowing that you should be doing something more meaningful?

8-Have a strong sense of right and wrong?

9- Do you get along with animals better than with people?

10-Do you have a knowing at times it is better to do the smart thing   instead of the right thing?

11- Do you have the ability to find solutions outside the framework of conventional   means?

12- Do you have a strong intolerance towards stupidity but have  deep compassion for others?

13- Do you have a burning desire to matter, to make your life count, to improve the world?

14- You didn't fit in at school, had issues with authority, found school to be boring?

15- Are you able to relate to children and the elderly bet ter than other groups?

16- Do you feel a connection to nature?

17- Do you prefer natural fabrics, cotton and wool, over synthetic fabrics, might be addicted to cashmere?

18- Do you have a hard time working in a structured envi ronment; prefer working alone or being in charge?

19- Do you have a knowing that the dogma of religion is manipulative and has a hidden agenda?

20- Do you have a high IQ, highly intelligent, although may not have made good grades in school?

21- Are you frustrated at the media for hiding an agenda?

22- Do you have a desire to seek out the truth on your own?

23- Do you refuse to accept anything without knowing the "Why" behind it?

24- Do you have a sense of anger and a feeling of being violated at your rights being taken away, concern and fear about Big Brother?

25- Are you very creative and inventive, and enjoy the arts, music, and literature?

26- Do you at times feel that no one understands or appre ciate you?

27- Do you have strong psychic abilities?

28- Do you feel that Michael Jackson was misunderstood?

29- Do you have a strong intuition?

30- Do you have a sense of "oneness" and a knowing of the connectedness to all life?

31- Have you had psychic experiences, premonitions, hearing voices, seeing Angels, or out of body experiences?

32- Do others consider you to be cynical?

33- Do you get very impatient with people when they don't get the point?

34- Do you have a desire to seek the meaning of Life?

35- At times, have you been extremely emotional or sensitive or at other times been the complete opposite?

36- Have you had trouble focusing on assignments?

37- Do you have a hard time buying into the American Dream?

38- Are your favorite colors blue and purple?

39- Do you have a deep intense longing for your Soul Mate, that one true love?

40- Are you in need of a lot of physical contact with your love one?

41- Do you have "trust" issues; have been betrayed in the past?

42- Did you grow up in a physically, emotionally, and spiritually abusive household?

43- Did you grow up around crime, physical abuse, sexual abuse, cults or mind control?

44- Do you go through periods of severe grief and loneliness?

45- Have you had issues with drugs or alcohol?

46- Do you prefer solo sports over team sports?

47- Prefer to be outside over being inside?

48- Are you or have been attracted to Martial Arts or sports that require discipline and self-defense?

49- Might have had issues with anger management?

50- At times, life seems painful for you?

51- Your abilities are not accepted or acknowledged?

52- Do you long for a place that feels like home?

53- Do you at times, have you felt abandoned and lost?

54- Do you at times wonder why you feel sad and depressed for no reason?

55- Do you feel that those closest to you don't know the real you?

56- You don't understand why you get it and others don't?

57- Have you had issues with your watch keeping time?

58- You seem to have difficulties with computers working properly?

59- Does it seem that you change a lot of light bulbs?

60- Do you have the ability to detect when you are being lied to?

61- At times, are you extremely critical to the point of being obsessive?

62- Are you empathic, able to sense and feel other peoples' emotions?

63- Are you sexually very expressive and active? Do you make it into an extreme sport? Or maybe you have no interest at all?

64- Did you have an interest in spiritual or psychic subjects at an early age?

65- Do you have a wisdom that is beyond your years?

66- Are you honest to a fault?

67- Do you tire easily and sleep longer than usual?

68- Do you have an intense dislike for conflict?

69- Do you dislike loud noise?

70- Are you a great multi-tasker?

71- Do you have memories of past lives?

72- At times, you have had an awareness of other dimen sions and parallel universes?

73- Do you get extremely focused on a project when moti vated?

74- Do you have this "knowingness" when it comes to cer tain subjects?

75- Do you have a fondness for movies like Knights Tale, Harry Potter, Kingdom of Heaven, Lord of the Rings, or movies with similar subjects?

Most Indigos will agree with at least 80% of the questions. If you fall into this group, good news, there are plenty of resources to dive into. At the end of this book is a resource page with several websites and books that you can check out. These will serve to further your journey to self discovery and becoming all that you are meant to be. If anything, do not be afraid to ask questions, ask and you will receive. Feel free to contact me with any questions or thoughts. We are all in this together and all a part of each other.

# Epilogue

## The Power Within, A Personal Message

You all have the power within to create any life you so desire. The only reason you are not living the life you desire or think that you deserve is because you don't believe that you have the power and belief that you control your life. This is not a secret, it is in plain view. Only your inability to believe this prevents you from this knowing. Open your eyes and see that you have the ability to create whatever life you desire. I don't care what your circumstances are, what your situation is, what kind of job you have, where you live, it doesn't matter. You are not your circumstances. You can decide today that you are not any of this. This isn't you. All of this is the results of the decisions and actions based on your previous belief system.

Today you can be armed with the tools to create the belief system that is your birthright. As Jesus said I am in you, you are in Me, and I am in the Father, whatever I can do you can do greater. This is the most empowering verse in the Bible. Just this one verse demonstrates that we are all God like. How can we not be Godlike if Jesus himself is telling us that he is within you and you within him? This is a knowing that must become the core of your belief. You must have faith that these words are true. Jesus said with faith the size of the mustard seed you could move mountains. He is telling you that you have the same powers as he. What is stopping you is the veil of illusion that creates the separation. The sense of separation comes from your belief that you are a human being in need of becoming a spiritual being through salvation. The reality is you are a spiritual being having a human experience. Once you rediscover that we are all part of God and believe this then you will be on the path to living the life of your desires. The salvation is in realizing that we are already part of Jesus, part of God and therefore part of the Source and Eternal Life.

## For Equilibrium - A Blessing by John O'Donohue

Like the Joy of the sea coming home to shore,
May the relief of Laughter rinse through your Soul.
As the wind loves to call things to Dance,
May your gravity by Lightened by Grace.
Like the Dignity of moonlight restoring the Earth,
May your thoughts incline with Reverence and Respect.

As water takes whatever shape it is in,
So free may you be about who you Become.
As Silence smiles on the other side of what's said,
May your sense of irony bring Perspective.
As time remains free of all that it frames,
May your mind stay Clear of all its names.
May your Prayer of Listening deepen enough
to Hear in the depths the laughter of God!

# Resource Page

**Victor Trucker** - www.perfect-oneness.com

**David Parke** - http://newyorkpastlife.com
http://coachingthesoul.com

**Daniel of Doria** - www.danielofdoria.com

**Kandice Bush** - www.thearchitectureofemotion.blogspot.com

# Books

Autobiography of a Yogi by Paramahansa Yoganada.

The Power of Intention by Dr. Wayne Dyer.

Inspiration, Your Ultimate Calling by Dr. Wayne Dyer.

Divine Matrix by Gregg Braden.

The Isaiah Effect by Gregg Braden.

Complete Idiot's Guide to Indigo Children by Wendy H. Chapman.

Black Elk Speaks by Black Elk as told to John G. Neihardt.

The Biology of Belief by Bruce Lipton PhD.

The Perennial Philosophy by Aldous Huxley.

Messages from Water by Doctor Masaru Emoto.

Thich Nhat Hanh, Essential Writings.

Terra Papers, by Robert Morning Sky.

190                                                         Are you an Indigo?

22541316R00109

Made in the USA
Middletown, DE
02 August 2015